STATISTICS FOR A MARKET ECONOMY

Edited by
Derek Blades

ORGANISATION FOR ECONOMIC CO-OPERATION AND DEVELOPMENT

Pursuant to Article 1 of the Convention signed in Paris on 14th December 1960, and which came into force on 30th September 1961, the Organisation for Economic Co-operation and Development (OECD) shall promote policies designed:

— to achieve the highest sustainable economic growth and employment and a rising standard of living in Member countries, while maintaining financial stability, and thus to contribute to the development of the world economy;
— to contribute to sound economic expansion in Member as well as non-member countries in the process of economic development; and
— to contribute to the expansion of world trade on a multilateral, non-discriminatory basis in accordance with international obligations.

The original Member countries of the OECD are Austria, Belgium, Canada, Denmark, France, Germany, Greece, Iceland, Ireland, Italy, Luxembourg, the Netherlands, Norway, Portugal, Spain, Sweden, Switzerland, Turkey, the United Kingdom and the United States. The following countries became Members subsequently through accession at the dates indicated hereafter: Japan (28th April 1964), Finland (28th January 1969), Australia (7th June 1971) and New Zealand (29th May 1973). The Commission of the European Communities takes part in the work of the OECD (Article 13 of the OECD Convention). Yugoslavia takes part in some of the work of the OECD (agreement of 28th October 1961).

Publié en français sous le titre :

STATISTIQUES
POUR UNE ÉCONOMIE DE MARCHÉ

The Centre for Co-operation with European Economies in Transition which was created in March 1990 is the focal point for co-operation between the OECD and central and eastern European countries. Its major responsibility is to design and manage a programme of policy advice and technical assistance which puts the expertise of the Secretariat and Member countries at the disposal of countries engaged in economic reform. This advice or assistance can take numerous forms, including conferences, seminars, missions and workshops in order to explore policy questions or review draft legislation; it can also include training for government officials who are called to implement market-oriented policies.

In December 1990 the OECD initiated a programme "Partners in Transition" for the purpose of providing more focused assistance to those countries that are more advanced in introducing market-oriented reforms and desire to become members of OECD. Additional activities, which the Centre would co-ordinate under this programme, could include reviews of the country's general economic situation and prospects, reviews of issues and policies in specific areas and participation in certain OECD committees.

In all these activities, the Centre maintains close relations with other multilateral bodies such as the G-24 co-ordinated by the Commission of the European Communities, the International Monetary Fund, the World Bank, the European Investment Bank, the European Bank for Reconstruction and Development, with the mutual objective of ensuring the complementarity of respective efforts to support economic reforms in Central and Eastern Europe.

Four activities in the Centre's current Work programme have been designated as part of the OECD's response to the invitation of the Bonn Conference of the CSCE to host meetings of experts from CSCE participating States and OECD Member States to promote the process of economic reform.

The Conference held in September dealing with the statistical systems, the proceedings of which are recorded in this volume, was the first of these activities. This volume will be followed by Centre publications related to the other activities, in particular the problems of the transition to a market-based system and the role of tax reform.

These proceedings were edited by Derek Blades, who is a statistician with the Economics and Statistics Department of the OECD.

The report is published on the responsibility of the Secretary-General of the OECD.

ALSO AVAILABLE

A Study of the Soviet Economy. Three volumes by the International Monetary Fund, The World Bank, Organisation for Economic Co-operation and Development, European Bank for Reconstruction and Development (1991)
(14 91 02 1) ISBN 92-64-13468-9 FF500 £50 US$100 DM148

The Economy of the USSR. Summary and Recommendations by the International Monetary Fund, the World Bank, Organisation for Economic Co-operation and Development and the European Bank for Reconstruction and Development (1990)
(14 91 01 1) ISBN 92-64-13453-0 FF80 £8.00 US$15.95 DM25

Cut along dotted line

ORDER FORM

Please enter my order for:

Qty.	*Title*	*Price*
....	....	....
....	....	....
....	....	....
....	....	....
	Total :	....

- Payment is enclosed ☐
- Charge my VISA card ☐ Number of card ....
  (Note: You will be charged the French franc price.)
  Expiration of card .... *Signature* ....
- *Send invoice. A purchase order is attached* ☐

Send publications to *(please print):*
Name ....
Address ....
....
....

Send this Order Form to OECD Publications Service, 2, rue André-Pascal, 75775 PARIS CEDEX 16, France, or to OECD Publications and Information Centre or Distributor in your country *(see last page of the book for addresses).*

Prices charged at the OECD Bookshop.

THE OECD CATALOGUE OF PUBLICATIONS and supplements will be sent free of charge on request addressed either to OECD Publications Service, or to the OECD Distributor in your country.

Table of Contents

I

Introduction and Summary of Discussions

Introduction

This volume is the first in a series of publications by the OECD Centre for Co-operation with European Economies in Transition. The purpose of this book, and those which will follow, is to add to understanding of the problems which the central and eastern European countries are, or will be, facing as they move from a centrally-planned to a market-oriented economy. The transformation of these economic systems is by both its nature and scale a task and an effort without precedent in our economic history. The lack of an adequate body of knowledge, from which governments can draw guidance, makes the transition all the more difficult, while the conditions of economic distress that characterise these countries at the beginning of the process make it all the more urgent. The co-operation and assistance of the prosperous market economies of the "West" could be crucial in avoiding such a transformation succumbing to the many difficulties.

Since late 1989, these reforming countries have been addressing requests for advice, co-operation and assistance to the OECD. The long history of the Organisation in supporting the development of market economies is one of the reasons for such requests. The OECD embodies, and perpetuates, the success of the co-operative experience of its predecessor, the Organisation for European Economic Co-operation (OEEC), established in 1948 to bolster the efforts of Western European countries in rebuilding their economies. In this endeavour a key factor was the support, through the Marshall Plan, of the United States of America.

The wealth of experience and expertise which the OECD and its Member countries can put at the disposal of the reforming countries in Central and Eastern Europe is considerable, covering as it does all the domains of economics as well as their interlinkages. Thus, the potential contribution of the OECD to the reform of those economies is unique.

In order to enable it to meet the growing number of requests by these countries, the OECD created, in March 1990, the Centre for Co-operation with the European Economies in Transition. The purpose of the Centre is to provide technical advice, to undertake policy dialogue and, in a few cases, to train officials in the context of a programme of activities that is designed and reviewed annually. The Centre is not established as a separate agency within the OECD but rather as an infrastructure that can rely on and mobilise the know-how both of the OECD staff and of its Member countries. Technical advice and policy dialogue take numerous forms and cover a wide range of subjects, spanning from macroeconomic issues to structural problems. Seminars, workshops and technical meetings are being held, involving on one side the OECD Secretariat, together with experts and policymakers from OECD countries, and on the other side, policymakers, officials and experts from Central and Eastern Europe. The experience of the business community is also called upon where appropriate. Specific policy questions are explored or draft legislation and administrative practices are reviewed. Furthermore, analyses of some economic sectors are being conducted in those countries. Training of government officials involved in implementing market-oriented policies is being carried out on a limited scale, for example in areas such as competition policy. In implementing its programme, the Centre maintains close relations with other multilateral institutions such as the International Monetary Fund, the World Bank and the EEC Commission, as well as with other multilateral programmes such as the G-24 programme that is co-ordinated by the EEC Commission.

The Centre's commitment to all these activities has been enhanced with the adoption of special programmes for co-operation in the context of the initiative "Partners in Transition" which was launched in December 1990. This initiative focuses on those countries in economic transition that are more advanced in the introduction of economic and social reforms and have expressed the intention of becoming members of the OECD. Each of these programmes is oriented towards the specific reform needs of a "partner in transition", and can also include the participation of these countries as an observer in the activities of certain OECD committees.

First steps in launching the Centre's activities must be to assess the extent and characteristics of the needs of the reforming economies, to understand what are the most appropriate instruments for support, and to establish the contribution being furnished by other institutions. As one means to this end, the Centre is sponsoring four major conferences. Each provides an opportunity to examine, with the representatives of the reforming countries, a specific set of issues in order to identify priorities for action and for international assistance in the transition to a market-based economy. These priorities can be expected to constitute the basis for developing specific activities which may be of interest to one or several of these countries. These conferences have also been designed as part of the OECD response to the invitation of the Bonn meeting of the Conference on Security and Co-operation in Europe to host meetings of experts from the CSCE participating States and OECD Member States to promote the process of economic reform.

The first conference, proceedings of which are reported in this volume, was held in September 1990, and dealt with the problem of reforming the countries' statistical systems. This subject was selected for the first conference because neither proper assessment of the economic situation nor good policy making are possible without the support of adequate quantitative information. The second conference, in November 1990, focused on the problems and difficulties of managing the economy in the transition to a market-system. The third conference, in January 1991, is devoted to the issues of tax reform, while the last conference of this cycle, in the summer of 1991, will examine the creation of a labour market and the social implications of the systemic reforms in Central and Eastern Europe.

Salvatore Zecchini
Director of
the Centre for Co-operation with
the European Economies in Transition

Opening Statement

by Salvatore Zecchini

Assistant Secretary-General and Director of the
Centre for Co-operation with the European Economies in Transition, OECD

It is time that I declare open the "Conference on the Statistics of Central and Eastern European Countries" that are on the way to establishing a new economic system based on free market forces and market mechanisms. I wish to start by thanking all of you for participating in this Conference. I am glad to see a diversified group of participants, including both producers of statistics and major users, with representatives coming from both the formerly centrally-planned economies and from the market economies, from governmental and research institutions and from national as well as international organisations. Among the latter, I have to pay a special tribute to the United Nations Economic Commission for Europe for sponsoring this Conference with us and for co-operating actively and effectively in pursuing our common goal – namely to have an exchange of analyses and experiences on issues that are crucial and pressing in the ongoing economic transformations in Central and Eastern Europe.

This Conference is the first major event of the programme of the OECD Centre for Co-operation with the European Economies in Transition. The Centre was created last March to respond in a systematic and structured way to the many requests for assistance that governments, faced with the mighty task of changing their political, social and economic systems, were making to the OECD. It is worth emphasising that this Organisation has underpinned the development of the European industrial economies since the end of the Second World War. The programme of activities of the Centre covers a broad range of economic areas extending from statistics to macroeconomic policies, market reform, technology transfer, regional development, and education. These are just some of the subject areas in which the Centre aims at transferring the knowledge and experience of the OECD Members to the reforming countries of Europe in order to support them in devising appropriate economic strategies, in implementing these in the most effective way and in monitoring their effects. To this end, the Centre makes use of a variety of instruments. In addition to conferences, the Centre organises policy discussions on a bilateral basis, technical workshops and seminars, direct technical assistance to governments on specific issues or on operational matters and offers a limited amount of training of public officials.

A distinctive feature of the OECD is that it can be the catalyst and the co-ordinator of inputs in terms of expertise and experience, deriving from both the Secretariat and our Member countries. In examining policy issues for decision making and particularly in dealing with radical reforms, there is no substitute for the experience of highly developed countries such as the OECD Members that have tested in their economies the validity of the solutions suggested by economic theories or by the econometric evidence. In making this experience available, the OECD also seeks inputs from other international institutions in the belief that, the tighter our co-operation, the more effective and comprehensive is the support that the advanced, industrial economies can provide to the reforming countries.

Among the various forms of assistance, the Centre sees this Conference, as well as three others which will follow in the coming months, as the necessary first step in a series of activities that will be developed in crucial policy areas over a number of years. Specifically, this and the other conferences will help to assess the extent of some of the main problems encountered in changing the command-type economic systems, to explore the multiple implications of this change, to harness a variety of contributions, to devise solutions, to elicit international co-operation and to allow better planning of external assistance in the future.

One might wonder why we start with a Conference on statistics. These countries have other more urgent problems such as food supplies, balance of payments, investment and enterprise restructuring. After all, quite a few people in both Eastern Europe and the West, when referring to statistics, are of the opinion that in our life we face three kinds of lies: lies, damned lies and statistics. Unfortunately, the quotation attributed to Mark Twain is not far from today's reality in several Central and Eastern European countries in which the official figures for, say, external debt, the rate of inflation or the growth of national product, are in strident contrast with the actual evidence of economic life. I presume that those who are present here share the view that instead of making up statistics, countries should look up to them as the prerequisite for proper decision-making in a free-market economy. It is not up to me to tell this group of distinguished experts how valuable statistics are. But I wish to touch briefly upon some aspects that should be kept in mind in the course of the following discussions.

Statistical data are only one element in the wider information framework that allows a market economy to work efficiently. This framework also includes elements aimed at identifying and measuring economic phenomena and behaviour, the ordering of all these elements in a reliable, summary form and the dissemination of such information. While in a planned economy the plan is at the centre of such a framework and generates statistical information in order to mould the economic reality of the country, in a market economy the market itself produces information. This takes place when the actions of market participants have an impact upon the determination of market prices, which in turn represent signals for the decisions of the authorities and economic agents. This is the underlying condition for an effective functioning of a market economy and it implies the abandonment of the normative type of statistical information that is inherent in central planning. In the latter's place there should emerge a system with pluralistic information sources that are related to the market place and mutually interacting. The establishment of such a system is a major challenge for the reformers of Central and Eastern Europe, but if this is not accomplished in the very early stages of economic reform, it is hard to conceive how a market economy can develop rapidly.

Without entering into a detailed examination of the requisites of this system, three questions deserve particular attention. First, what features are most relevant for statistics in a market economy? Second, towards the needs of which sectors should statistics be oriented? Third, what use to make of the statistics?

As to the characteristics of statistics for a market economy, two seem crucial to me: nominal values and reliability. First, it is evident that regardless of whether an economy is centrally planned or market based, economic statistics are essential for economic management. In the former system, however, physical quantity data are of paramount importance, and because they lack a common value denominator and involve insolvable aggregation problems they tend to blur the vision of the whole of the economy. In a market economy, on the other hand, the measurement of values or the monetary expression of economic phenomena needs to be emphasized and fully developed. Second, the reliability of statistics is determinant for making good decisions. Almost paradoxically, many statistics in a market economy are not accounting records but stochastic statements. They have a hidden stochastic error that is often unidentifiable. In such a context, the value of statistics for the economy depends crucially on **not** being systematically biased in order to serve some particular purpose, i.e. their value depends on lying close to the middle of the error range. In this respect, Jaroslav Jilek rightly underscores in his paper the problem of restoring confidence in the statistics of these reforming economies after years during which suppliers, compilers and users conspired to "improve" data on plan achievements.

As to the orientation of statistical services, the needs of all the main groups of economic agents – households, enterprises and government deserve attention. Since governments directly fund the main statistical agencies, their data requirements are usually the first to be satisfied. Even if governments' needs are privileged, they should not be exclusive in guiding the supply of statistical services. In a market economy, the enterprise and household sectors are the driving force of economic development by operating in competitive markets and they need statistics to deal with the uncertainties of markets and economic behaviour. The government itself, once it is prevented from imposing its choices on the economic behaviour of economic actors, must gather more statistical information on the choices of enterprises and households to plan and assess the impact of its indirect interventions.

With respect to the use of statistics, dissemination of data together with freedom of economic information-gathering are essential to prevent market failure. Of course, the other preconditions to avoid market failure are that markets exist and fulfill their informational role by allowing a large number of market participants to transfer their information into the determination of prices under competitive conditions. The market system functions at its best when all economic actors have at their disposal the maximum of information. In fact, however, good information is scarce and unevenly distributed among market participants, with the result that the effectiveness of market mechanisms in spurring and guiding economic development is hampered. It is the responsibility of the government to help overcome these obstacles and this implies, first, giving the public access to economic information through recognition of the right to information. Second, the government itself should consider supplying a critical mass of statistics and informational elements as a "public good" that is available to all without discrimination.

Transforming a centrally-planned economy into a market-based one mainly involves granting freedom of economic choice, but this freedom would be deprived of much of its meaning if the subject of this choice is not given the possibility of acquiring an adequate degree of knowledge of the terms of his or her choice. Dissemination of statistics therefore plays a fundamental role both in economic liberalisation and in ensuring market success. Beyond the economic realm, the diffusion of statistics serves social and political purposes. The more people know about the economic and social realities of their country, the better are they equipped to make proper use of their right to determine the policies of their country, thereby strengthening democracy. Krystof Hegemejer rightly emphasises this point. He notes that from its earliest days the Solidarity trade union in Poland demanded access to a broad range of statistics. Suspicious of the official price index, Solidarity even compiled its own index by conducting its own household budget surveys and price collection.

Apart from these aspects, I must stress the importance of focusing some of the discussions of this Conference on the statistics that are most relevant to help policy makers in designing and implementing a strategy for the transition to a market system. This is the main challenge the reforming countries are facing at present and this Conference will miss a major objective if it were not to allow an extensive and deep discussion of the statistical issues for crucial policy making in the process of transforming these economies.

Before concluding, a few words on the contribution of the OECD in the field of statistics. In this area our Organisation has fulfilled two main tasks: to devise international standards for the compilation and presentation of statistics in co-operation with other major international institutions; and to publish a wide range of useful statistics on its Member countries. With respect to statistical standards, the OECD encourages its Members to adopt best practices and to ensure international comparability of their data. Comparability of data on economic and social performance is a necessary condition for the OECD to pursue one of its main objectives, namely to enable the OECD Member countries to assess the effects of different economic policy approaches for the purpose of improving them. In this context the OECD has played a leading role in developing international standards for statistics on national accounts, the labour force, taxes and public subsidies, energy balances, research and development expenditures, the services sector, the environment and purchasing power parities. As to the dissemination of statistics, the OECD has never been a "passive" publisher, content merely to reproduce the data provided by its Members. Before publication, data are carefully scrutinised to ascertain that they are properly compiled and as reliable as possible.

Finally, a word on the structuring of the Conference. The first substantive session of the Conference will debate the needs for statistical information of users ranging from government to the business community, research institutes, trade unions and international organisations. Subsequent sessions will focus on the statistics supplied by the statistical agencies of the Central and Eastern European countries. They will also deal with ways and means by which these agencies could adjust their work programmes to effectively meet the information requirements of policy makers that are engaged in transforming their economic systems.

The final session will be devoted to the contributions of national and international institutions to assist the reforming countries in upgrading their statistical services. As to the OECD, assistance by the Centre might take several forms such as the organisation of working groups, seminars, traineeships in OECD departments and technical missions in the reforming countries. It is our hope that at the end of this Conference, we will not only reach a better understanding of the issues under examination but also lay the foundations for more rational co-operation, if not co-ordination, among the various suppliers of assistance in the field of statistics.

Conference Report

Derek Blades

Economics and Statistics Department

I. Introduction

The Conference on Statistics of Central and Eastern European countries was organised by the OECD **Centre for Co-operation with the European Economies in Transition** and cosponsored by the UN **Economic Commission for Europe.** It was held at the OECD in Paris from the 10th to the 12th September 1990.

One hundred and fifty outside participants attended the Conference. They represented a wide range of users and producers of statistics from virtually all OECD countries and from seven countries in Central and Eastern Europe – Bulgaria, the Czech and Slovak Federal Republic, East Germany, Hungary, Poland, Romania and the Soviet Union. Yugoslavia, which began its transition to a market system some years ago, also took part.

II. Background

The aim of the Conference was to consider how statistical offices in Central and Eastern European countries will need to adapt their outputs and procedures to meet the new policy requirements that will arise as these countries replace central planning by market mechanisms. In the Central and Eastern European countries (CEECs), government statistical offices have traditionally played a very different role from that of their counterparts in OECD countries. The transition from central planning to market systems does not merely imply that different kinds of statistics are required. It involves a full-scale rethinking both of working practices in statistical offices and of the way that government statisticians perceive their role in society.

There are clearly many differences between the CEECs in their social and economic institutions and these differences are reflected in the attitudes and outputs of their statistical agencies. In particular, Poland and Hungary have incorporated many western features into their statistical services in recent years. In Poland, for example, an independent review body was set up to review the work of the Central Statistical Office at the beginning of the 1980s and Hungary has virtually abandoned the Material Product System for reporting national accounts statistics to international agencies in favour of the OECD's System of National Accounts. However, while it is dangerous to generalise, it is useful to make some general remarks on the way that statistical offices in these countries have been operating for most of the last forty years in order to gauge the extent of the changes that are now required.

In most of the countries of Central and Eastern Europe, the principal function of the statistical offices was to monitor the central plans. These plans prescribed detailed production targets for each state-owned enterprise and statistical offices were required to oversee the progress of each enterprise in meeting the plan targets. Statistical offices behaved, in effect, like state auditors exercising regular and detailed supervision of the operations of the state enterprises. This auditing role had a number of implications both for their working methods and for the kinds of statistics that they collected.

First, since plans were drawn up in physical terms, statistical offices collected relatively few data expressed in monetary terms. Their statistical publications are largely devoted to documenting volumes produced and give little or no information on values, costs and prices. In describing their future plans the USSR, Poland and Romania all emphasise the need to develop these new kinds of statistics.

Secondly, since each enterprise had its own production target, the statistical offices were required to keep track of each and every one. In contrast to OECD countries where sample surveys are the standard practice, virtually all statistical enquiries in the CEECs were complete censuses. This explains the emphasis now given by participants from these countries to developing sample survey techniques and, equally important, to learning how to win cooperation from respondents who will now enjoy much greater autonomy than in the past. It also explains the large size of statistical offices in most CEECs where enormous numbers of questionnaires had to be processed – usually with data processing equipment that would be considered inadequate by western standards.

Thirdly, in acting as the interface between the enterprises and the planners, statistical offices in the CEECs were often under pressure to compromise their professional standards. The planning offices wanted to be assured that the targets they had prescribed were being met and the statistical offices had more interest in reporting successes than failures. "Successes" were also important for reporting enterprises since they could lead to bonus payments. At the very least, it is clear that statistical offices had little incentive to verify reports that showed enterprises fulfilling their plan targets even if they suspected that they may be unduly optimistic, while they were likely to query reports of short-falls.

In addition to their role as auditors, statistical offices in CEECs were also expected to perform a propaganda function. Seeing themselves in an adversarial role vis-à-vis the West, governments in CEECs used statistics to bolster assertions that centrally-planned systems were more successful than market economies in raising living standards. Since, as is now generally recognised, such assertions were simply not true, the statistical offices in these countries were under continuous pressure to present social and economic developments in the best possible light. Sometimes this lead to outright falsification of data; more generally it lead to suppression of unwelcome statistics or to presentation of data in misleading or uninformative ways. Data suppression was widespread in the German Democratic Republic and in Romania; the latter virtually stopped publishing statistics in the mid-1980s. A common example of misleading presentation is the publication of rates of change using carefully selected base periods to produce "true" but nevertheless exaggerated impressions of growth.

Another common feature is that there are frequent breaks in time series either because of changes to base years or because of changes in methodology. These breaks were often introduced without alerting users. While it may be true that long time series were not necessary for the all-important function of monitoring the five-yearly plans, the suspicion remains that at least some statistical offices introduced breaks in time series deliberately to prevent objective analysis of long-term trends which would have contradicted official assertions of steady progress in achieving social and economic goals.

It was against this background of outdated methods, inappropriate statistics, low credibility and questionable publication policies that the Conference turned to consideration of data needs. What kinds of new statistics will be required in the CEECs for policy purposes by users in government, in business, in trade unions, in international organisations and by analysts in research institutes and universities?

III. Data requirements for policy purposes

In the OECD countries, markets dictate statistical programmes and since markets operate in similar ways in all countries, statistical offices in OECD countries publish a very similar range of economic statistics. In consequence, it is fairly simple to identify the broad subject areas where statistical agencies in CEECs will need to develop new or improved statistics. Chief among these are national accounts, prices, labour force and foreign trade statistics. Monetary and financial statistics will also need to be developed as the unitary banking systems in the CEECs are converted to a market basis. The problem, however, is that identification of broad subject areas is not in itself very helpful. The important and more difficult task is to pin-point the specific data sets that users most urgently need within these broader areas.

National accounts provide a good example. There is widespread agreement that the CEECs should adopt, as a matter of urgency, the OECD-UN System of National Accounts (SNA), but the SNA is a very broad and comprehensive system. It covers both stocks and flows, it includes an input-output framework and a flow-of-funds matrix and it touches virtually all aspects of economic activity. It is simply not practical to recommend the CEECs to implement the system in its entirety: a selective approach is required. Labour force statistics, which all users identified as a priority, provide another example. Trade unions and some other users would ideally like labour force data to be cross-classified by industry, occupation, sex and age but it would be unrealistic to demand this amount of detail, at least on a monthly or quarterly basis. Here again, selectivity is essential. The papers submitted for this session, the comments of the discussants and the subsequent discussions served to identify the **core needs** of users in these and other areas.

For **national accounts**, priority needs consist of final expenditures on the GDP at current and constant prices and the income and outlay accounts for government, households and enterprises. All these data should be compiled according to the SNA. As regards **labour force statistics**, employment by broad industry groups and unemployment by sex and broad age groups are the essential requirements. Two kinds of **price indices** were considered essential – one for producers' prices and the other for consumer prices. The latter are sometimes compiled separately for strategic groups of consumers – low-paid urban households, retired persons, rural households etc. Experience of users in OECD countries confirms that it is usually better to have a single index based on the average expenditure patterns of the nation as a whole. As soon as more than one consumer price index is published, pressures grow for additional indices targeted at other groups. Wage bargaining and other adjustments for inflation then become sterile arguments about which index is the more appropriate. **Indices of industrial production** can be confined to a total index combining extraction, manufacturing and construction industries plus a component index for manufacturing and possibly one for construction. In general, the essential needs of most users can be satisfied by a limited number of highly aggregated statistics. There is always a market for more elaborate and more detailed economic data but when resources are limited – as they clearly are in the statistical offices of the CEECs – the most efficient way to proceed is to concentrate on a small number of aggregative statistics of the kind mentioned above.

It was suggested that more elaborate statistics which are needed by particular users could sometimes be assembled by the users themselves. For example, trade unions engaged in collective bargaining may require very detailed information about working conditions of specific groups of employees. In several OECD countries, the trade unions work with enterprise managers to compile agreed sets of data for joint use by the bargaining partners.

In considering users needs, frequent reference was made to international standards. Implementation of international **systems** such as the OECD-UN System of National Accounts or the IMF Balance of Payments and Government Finance systems and the adoption of international **nomenclatures** such as the UN foreign trade and industry classifications clearly aid international comparisons. The growing importance of international comparability was emphasised by participants from the business sector and trade unions. But the adoption of international systems brings another important advantage. These standards are designed to reflect "best practices", so that by adopting them countries are encouraged to improve their own data sources and methods of compilation.

Several speakers noted that data needs may be rather different during the "transition periods" than when the CEECs will have achieved market-based economies. Potentially therefore, there is a conflict between short and long term aims. There was a consensus that statistical agencies should devote the greater part of their resources to the longer term objective – that is, to developing the kind of statistical system that will best serve their countries when they have finally become market-economies.

At the same time, it was recognised that statistical agencies in CEECs had an important role in aiding and abetting the transition process itself. To achieve this latter objective, policy makers would have particular need of up to date information on short-term developments in the business sector and on the economic and social situation of households. "Business surveys", which seek information on the present and future intentions of business managers were agreed to be well suited to meeting the first requirement. They are relatively cheap to conduct, several CEECs already have some experience with them and they are widely used in OECD countries. To obtain key data on households – specifically incomes, expenditures and saving – statistical agencies in the CEECs may need to substantially enhance their "survey capability". There are several aspects to this capability – a trained body of interviewers, experience in questionnaire design and sample selection, and the administrative skills rapidly to implement surveys where and when they are required and to process and publish the results while they may still influence the policy-making process.

IV. Data now available for the Central and Eastern European Countries

Several participants noted that there was substantially more economic data available for the CEECs than suggested in some of the OECD Secretariat papers prepared for the Conference. The problem was that until recently there had been many restrictions on publication of economic and social statistics of a kind which were widely disseminated in OECD countries. This was now changing. Romania, for example, which had published virtually no economic statistics for the last 5 years, has now reintroduced regular, statistical publications. Data that had been compiled but not published during this blank period were now being released.

Particular attention was given to national accounting statistics. One participant reported that from a recent survey he had found that, for all CEECs except Albania, current price estimates of GDP have been compiled according to the SNA. These data cover at least the 1980s. However, relatively few CEECs have compiled GDP data at constant prices.

Other participants stressed that the Material Product System (MPS) was a valid accounting system. Although more limited in scope than the SNA, MPS data may contain a somewhat lower "guess-factor" than the SNA. While all the CEECs are now committed to introducing the SNA, MPS accounts should be retained during the transition to SNA. Statisticians from several CEECs confirmed that this was indeed their intention.

The Conference considered problems in using national accounts statistics whether they are compiled according to the MPS or the SNA. The term "detrimental growth" was applied to past attempts by CEECs to increase aggregates such as GDP or NMP. These attempts had led to the maximisation of output regardless of whether there was a market for the commodities produced. The goods may be of such poor quality that they were added to stocks of goods that were virtually unsaleable, but which nevertheless boosted recorded output. Alternatively, consumers may be forced to buy them because nothing else was on offer. Growth had also been detrimental in many CEECs because the accounting systems do not count environmental degradation and resource depletion as costs.

International comparisons of GDP and related aggregates suffer from particular problems in CEECs. Exchange rates are widely recognised as unsatisfactory convertors for international comparisons even in OECD countries whose currencies are freely convertible. In CEECs, currencies are usually non-convertible and there may be multiple exchange rates. For these reasons several CEECs have participated in various phases of the UN International Comparison Project to calculate Purchasing Power Parities (PPPs). The USSR, the Czech and Slovak Federal Republic, Hungary, Poland and Yugoslavia will all take part in the 1990 round of comparisons.

Another approach to international comparisons of GDP is the "Physical Indicator" (PI) method. The relationship between GDP and indicators of physical output is calculated for a sample of countries that use the SNA as their main system. Assuming that this relationship also applies to the CEECs, GDP estimates can then be obtained from their statistics on physical output.

In discussing the relative merits of the PI and PPP methods, it was noted that the relationships between GDP and physical indicators was rather unstable both over time and between countries. On the other hand, there are special problems in PPP comparisons for CEECs because it is often difficult to find goods and services of the same quality in the CEECs and the other countries. It was suggested that for this reason PPPs for CEECs may be systematically overstated. The consensus was that the PPP approach is generally to be preferred, but the PI method has the advantage that it can be applied to countries that are unwilling, or unable, to devote the not inconsiderable resources required to calculate PPPs.

The transition from a command economy to a market basis will not only affect the levels and growth rates of economic statistics but also their interpretation. The process should involve the production of new "goods" in the place of old "bads" such as unsaleable goods and inefficient services. But this genuine improvement in economic welfare may show up as lower or even stagnant growth in the national accounts. It was therefore suggested that it may be futile to attempt to construct long time series spanning the pre- and post-transition periods. While there was some sympathy with this view it was also recognised that analysts do demand long time series and that they will construct them themselves – often using inferior methods – if they are not supplied by the official statistical agencies.

V. Development strategies for statistics

Public image

There was, first, a discussion about how to improve the public image of statistical agencies in the CEECs and public acceptance of their statistics. In many CEECs, the role of the statistical agencies in monitoring the implementation of the central plan has had a pernicious effect on statistical morality. Sometimes official statisticians conspired with managers of state enterprises to "improve" data to show that plan targets were being achieved. One participant described this as "self-lying": both the providers and the collectors of statistics had colluded in falsifying the statistics and yet both behaved as though they believed them to be true. Because they had no independent status, many statistical offices had been required to be highly selective in publishing their data. Statistics that cast an unfavourable light on economic and social developments were not published or were presented in ways that made it difficult to draw the appropriate conclusions.

Publications policy was identified as an important area in the quest to establish public credibility. All CEECs should, like all OECD countries, publish regular, preferably monthly, reports on current economic statistics. The data included therein must be released at regular and pre-determined intervals even though publication at that time may sometimes be politically inconvenient. This is the clearest possible demonstration of the political independence of the statistical agency.

Public confidence in official statistics can be greatly enhanced by establishing an independent group of key users to review the work programme of the statistical office.

In some OECD countries these bodies have been set up to review work on particularly sensitive statistics, notably prices and labour force statistics. In other countries, review bodies have responsibilities over the entire statistical programme. This was the preferred model since this not only serves the aim of maintaining public confidence but will also help to ensure that the statistics collected by the national statistical office correspond to the needs of the main users. Review bodies should include representatives from trade unions, business organisations and independent analysts as well as officials from the main user agencies within government.

The extent of public disillusionment with official statistics varied widely between CEECs but it was suggested that in some cases public confidence could only be restored by appointing some kind of "prestige commission", consisting of internationally respected experts who would examine current statistical practices, define priority needs and recommend how public confidence could be restored. The appointment of such a commission would signal a clear break with the past and provide a public demonstration that the role of the statistical agency was undergoing a radical change.

Cooperation with respondents

In reforming their statistical organisations, the CEECs can learn from OECD experience. Participants from statistical offices in OECD countries explained how they maintain cooperative arrangements with their data suppliers. It is particularly important to win the trust and cooperation of enterprises. The statistical office must keep in touch with enterprises at all stages of the data collection process. Questionnaires should be designed in cooperation with enterprises or with trade organisations that represent their interests, and statistical publications should be designed to meet the needs of the enterprise sector as well as those of policy-makers. Some OECD statistical offices repay their respondents with special tabulations showing the data submitted by each enterprise together with aggregated statistics for other enterprises in the same industry. It was also noted that information collected in "Business Surveys", which report managers' assessments of the current situation and their expectations for the immediate future, are of particular interest to the enterprise sector.

Administrative data sources

The CEECs can also learn from mistakes made by OECD statistical offices. In particular, they should ensure that administrative data – company accounts, tax returns, social security records, customs documents and unemployment registers, for example – are designed to serve statistical as well as administrative purposes. The extensive revision of administrative procedures now being undertaken in several CEECs provides statistical offices with a unique opportunity to ensure that administrative records of this kind can also serve statistical purposes. Administrative records are often an alternative to statistical enquiries and their use by statistical offices can significantly reduce the reporting burden on enterprises and, to a lesser extent, on households.

Planned improvements

Representatives from the CEECs explained their present plans for reform. Although there were differences of emphasis there was broad agreement on the main elements of their development strategies. All recognise that for several years they will need a **mixed system**; a good part of the existing statistical programme will have to be kept in place as new, market-oriented statistics are gradually introduced. All recognise that the privatisation of state enterprises will involve a drastic overhaul of their **data collection procedures**. Enterprises will no longer regard provision of detailed statistics as a necessary part of their functions and will have to be persuaded to cooperate; at the same time, the rapid growth of the private sector is creating substantial extra work in maintaining accurate business registers which are a prerequisite for sample surveys. Most recognise that it is essential to improve their information on **prices**, and all recognise that this will become increasingly difficult as price controls are dismantled. All intend to adopt the **international systems** used by OECD countries – notably the System of National Accounts and the standard trade and industry classifications. Finally, they recognise that they have an important extra task in establishing new methods for compiling **foreign trade statistics** as the present trade monopolies are dismantled.

Planned reductions

These new tasks will impose considerable demands on statistical organisations that already consider themselves to be over-worked and under-staffed. Clearly, new work can only be undertaken if existing work is reduced. The Conference considered what kinds of statistics presently compiled in CEECs could be dropped to make way for new market-oriented statistics. Each country will need to decide this for itself but output statistics were identified as an area where substantial savings could be made in most CEECs. Detailed statistics on output in physical terms will become largely superfluous as central planning is abandoned. Statistics on gross output in value terms are often compiled at several different levels of aggregation – establishment, enterprise and concern, for example. In future, these statistics will only be needed for the statistical unit that is adopted for compiling the production accounts. Usually this will be the establishment.

Another group of statistics that can be reduced or even dropped are the various analytic statistics that were introduced to overcome the inefficiencies that are inherent in a centrally-planned economy. For example, because managers were not required to maximise profits, a number of special efficiency indicators have been introduced in several CEECs. These include indicators of labour turnover, energy consumption ratios and asset utilisation rates. Again, because of the emphasis on production rather than sales, a number of detailed inventory statistics have had to be introduced to identify surplus and unsaleable stocks of finished goods.

As well as scaling down and, in many cases, abandoning existing statistics, resources can be released for new work by simplifying data collection procedures. The use of sample surveys instead of complete censuses is an obvious example. Savings can also come from dropping the distinction between material and non-material output. This distinction greatly complicates data processing in statistical offices and also imposes a considerable burden on enterprises. In order to make the distinction accurately, respondents in large enterprises were often required to construct a set of miniature input-output tables.

VI. Special topics

In its fourth session the Conference discussed a number of "special topics". These were areas of statistical work which the Conference organisers believed to be of particular interest to the CEECs and where the OECD and other international organisations might be able to provide technical guidance and other types of assistance. This session dealt with methods to improve survey-response, price statistics, national accounts, leading indicators of business activity, energy statistics, purchasing power parities and statistics of government revenues.

Survey response

Hitherto, enterprises in CEECs have regarded statistical reporting as an obligatory part of their functions and very high response rates have been characteristic of industrial and enterprise surveys in CEECs. Statisticians in these countries expect this to change because they will have difficulties both in keeping track of the new private enterprises that are now being created and, once they have been located, in ensuring that they reply to surveys. On this latter problem, statisticians from OECD countries agreed that although laws may provide legal penalties for non-response, it was almost never adviseable to apply legal sanctions. High response rates are best achieved through "relevance and thoughtfulness". Enterprises are more likely to reply to a survey if they can see why they are being asked to supply the information requested. It was noted that it is usually unwise to ask a business for information which it does not collect for its own purposes; if the information is not relevant for its own operations the enterprise will not see why the government needs it.

Reducing the reporting burden on enterprises is an important objective. Obviously sample surveys rather than complete censuses should be used, and samples should be randomly selected with probability proportional to size. ("Size" will usually be defined by reference to gross output, turnover or employment). In this way only a small percentage of the smallest enterprises need to be surveyed and it is these enterprises which are least able and willing to complete questionnaires. It is also advisable to use simpler questionnaires for small and medium sized enterprises asking for less detailed information on a small number of key variables.

Participants were unanimous in recommending the maximum use of data from administrative sources – notably company accounts and tax returns. This could make it possible entirely to eliminate some types of surveys or to drop certain kinds of businesses (e.g. small ones) from the survey. It had been noted in an earlier session that the CEECs now have a unique opportunity to influence the design of administrative reporting methods to ensure that statistical requirements were not overlooked.

Price indices

Price indices are crucial statistics for the CEECs. The adoption of market mechanisms is certain to result in sharp movements in relative prices and the reduction in subsidies will cause some rise in the general price level. The CEECs face two main problems in the transition period – calculation of price indices on a monthly basis instead of quarterly or annually and adjustment of weighting patterns following sharp changes in relative prices. Monthly publication of a reliable and representative consumer price index is clearly a key task for official statistical agencies in countries that are considering frequent indexation of wages and pensions.

Two difficulties peculiar to CEECs were discussed. In some countries, consumer goods sold at low prices by state enterprises are resold at higher prices on a private basis. In such cases, which transaction should be for use in calculating the consumer price index? Participants agreed that the higher, private sale, prices should be used because these were the prices paid by the final consumers; the lower, state sector, prices were for intermediate transactions between traders and were not relevant for a consumer price index. The other difficulty concerns shortages. As shortages can be regarded as a form of hidden or "suppressed" inflation, it was suggested that indices might be calculated using estimated prices high enough to reduce demand to the available supply.

National accounts

Two main points emerged from the discussion about national accounts. All CEECs have now agreed to replace the Material Product System (MPS) by the System of National Accounts (SNA). While it is generally agreed that this is a wise decision because the SNA is more widely used at the international level than the MPS and because the SNA is a much more comprehensive system, several participants emphasised that the adoption of the SNA would not, in itself, solve the statistical problem of the CEECs. National accounts statistics, whether compiled according to the MPS or the SNA, are only as good as the basic information underlying them. MPS statistics are unsatisfactory in several countries because of inadequate or inaccurate basic statistics. This was the real problem facing the CEECs and would have to be addressed regardless of which accounting system was used.

The Conference considered at some length the role and use of input-output tables, which are included in both the SNA and the MPS. There was disagreement between participants from OECD countries about the priority to be assigned to input-output statistics. Some OECD countries compile these statistics on an annual basis, and regard the input-output matrix as an essential device for checking the consistency of the basic data. Others compile input-output tables only every five years or so and do not regard them as an essential – or even very useful – part of the system. Both groups include countries with long, and even pioneering, traditions in the field of national accounts.

Aside from the role of input-output statistics as a means of compiling national accounts, consideration was given to their use in economic analysis. In OECD countries they serve mainly for historical analysis and research. They are rarely used directly for current economic analysis, although they are sometimes used to estimate parameters for econometric models, such as consumption or import propensities. Participants from the CEECs noted that the constant technology assumptions which underlie most input-output analysis are likely to be invalidated by the radical transformation of their economies now under way. It was also stated that although input-output techniques are generally believed to be useful for formulating central plans, in practice relatively little use had been made of input-output tables in most CEECs.

The other topics included in this session had been introduced mainly to inform participants from the CEECs about areas of statistical work where the OECD Secretariat had special interest and expertise. There was further discussion on only two of the topics – leading indicators and purchasing power parities.

Leading indicators

The OECD Secretariat has developed a set of leading indicators for its Member countries which predict changes in the direction and pace of growth of industrial production. Two possible difficulties were noted in constructing leading indicators for the CEECs. First, the transition from a planned to a market economy is likely drastically to change behavioural relationships so that economic series found to have good prediction characteristics in the pre-transition years may no longer have them during and after the transition. Second many of the economic series commonly used as leading indicators for the OECD countries were not yet available in many CEECs. Financial variables such as interest rates, share prices and money supply, and qualitative "business climate" statistics which are obtained from "Business Surveys", are only available for a few CEECs and then only for a few years.

It was agreed, however, that even if reliable leading indicators cannot be constructed in the immediate future, CEECs would be well-advised to initiate programmes of business surveys. These produce data which are useful immediately even if it will be some years before long enough time series become available to use them for constructing leading indicators. It was noted that in several OECD countries, business surveys are carried out by private trade organisations, chambers of commerce, or non-government research bodies. Business surveys are not necessarily a responsibility of the official statistical agencies.

Purchasing power parities

The OECD Secretariat has participated, in close cooperation with the Statistical Office of the European Communities, in bench-mark calculations of purchasing power parities (PPPs) for 1980 and 1985, and it is now engaged on the calculation of PPPs for 1990 for all OECD Member countries. It was noted that overall and component PPPs are of considerable interest in their own right for price analysis, that they are relevant for exchange-rate policy – particularly in a country like the USSR which presently has multiple and widely different exchange rates – and that, above all, PPPs make it possible to compare directly levels of output and income between countries. Participants from a few OECD countries, while accepting that PPPs had many potential uses in policy-making, argued that participation in the PPP programme was expensive and suggested that it might not be a first-order priority. Other participants noted that an increasing number of CEECs are now taking part in the European

"Group II" PPP programme, which is based on bilateral comparisons with Austria. Statisticians from the CEECs place particular value on the PPP programme because it involves intensive "learning by doing" in working with colleagues from OECD countries both on price statistics and on national accounts compiled according to the SNA.

VII. Priorities for statistical development and role of the OECD

In the final session, the Conference considered what, in the light of user needs, should be considered as priority tasks for statistical offices in the CEECs, and what role the OECD and other international organisations could play in helping them realise their new objectives.

In considering priorities, participants from the CEECs were invited to speak first, followed by OECD country participants. Priorities were considered first with regard to **infrastructure** – data collection methods, publications policy, access to administrative records and so on – and secondly with regard to **statistical outputs.**

Infrastructure

In all CEECs, the creation of a private enterprise sector, through privatisation, demonopolisation of state enterprises and the creation of new private companies, presents statistical offices with major new problems which they feel ill-equipped to solve. Almost all CEEC participants identified as a priority task the establishment of **business registers** to keep track of the changing production structure. Most CEECs also mentioned **survey methodology** as a priority area; compulsory censuses of households, enterprises and government departments will need to be replaced by sample surveys and CEEC statistical offices will have to learn new skills in designing sample surveys and user-friendly questionnaires.

Statistical offices in CEECs would like to make maximum use of **administrative records** as an alternative to statistical surveys of enterprises.

Participants from several CEECs therefore mentioned **business accounting** as a priority area. The problem here is to ensure that the new rules for business accounting, which are now being drawn up in many CEECs, will provide data on production, financial and distributive transactions as these are defined in the SNA and other international statistical standards.

The adoption of **international classifications** was identified as a priority area by several CEECs. To maintain comparability with historical series, conversion tables will need to be further developed; this was seen as a task for the international organisations, particularly the United Nations and the Council for Mutual Economic Cooperation.

Still under the infrastructure heading, Romania mentioned the improvement of **publications** as a high priority and Poland mentioned the need to improve the **timeliness** of price indices and other key short term statistics. Timeliness may well emerge as a priority for other CEECs as the pace of transition accelerates: in many cases data which are routinely available on a monthly basis in OECD Countries are presently published only quarterly or annually in the CEECs.

In commenting on these infrastructure issues, participants from OECD countries supported the use of administrative records as a cheap and effective alternative to surveys. Some reserves were expressed about the use of administrative records for measuring unemployment, but there was unanimity that CEECs should fully exploit their present opportunity to influence business accounting rules so that company accounts could serve as substitutes for enterprise surveys to the maximum extent possible. The OECD participants agreed that this was an area where the CEECs could avoid the mistakes made in their own countries where business accounting rules were established without regard to statistical requirements.

Statistical offices would, of course, always have to carry out some surveys. In most cases, however, they should be sample surveys with cluster and stratification methods used to reduce their size and cost. CEECs were also advised to minimise the amount of detail requested from respondents.

As regards the establishment of business registers, OECD participants warned against their proliferation. In an ideal world, there would be a single register and every enterprise (and even more ideally every person) would have a single identity number which remained with them for life and which would be used by the banks, the statistical office, the tax administration and other government agencies.

Finally, there was strong encouragement from OECD participants for regular and more frequent publication of short term statistics. CEECs should aim at monthly publication of statistics on prices, output, employment, unemployment and related short-term variables.

Statistical outputs

As regards statistical outputs, participants were invited to distinguish between short-term and longer-term priorities. Participants from CEECs were unanimous in identifying **price statistics** as a high priority in the short-term. Both "producer price" as well as "consumer price" indices were mentioned. Most CEECs already publish price indices but they now face priority tasks in switching from a quarterly to a monthly basis and in expanding price collection beyond state and cooperative firms to the growing private sector.

The two other short-term priorities most often mentioned were statistics on **wages** and on **unemployment**. Some data on wages are already collected by all CEECs but these currently cover only the socialised sector and will need to be extended to private companies. Unemployment statistics have rarely been compiled by CEECs in the past. They urgently need to start preparing such data and most indicated that they will use survey methods (as recommended by the international organisations) rather than replying on administrative records from public labour offices.

For the longer term, high priorities were assigned by most CEECs to **national accounts, foreign trade statistics, balance of payments, government revenue data and financial statistics** such as interest rates, money supply and domestic credit.

All CEECs are now committed to introducing the System of National Accounts (SNA). The problem is to identify the priority parts of what is a very comprehensive system touching virtually all aspects of economic activity. Most CEECs that addressed this issue put high priority on current and constant price estimates of final expenditure on GDP and the income and outlay accounts for government, households and enterprises.

Participants from OECD countries and the international organisations generally agreed with this ordering of priorities for statistical outputs. However, some suggested that business surveys should also be considered a high priority area. It was also suggested that monetary and banking statistics will soon become a priority area although not necessarily for statistical offices; central banks would generally be responsible for such data.

It was emphasised that to make room for these new statistics, statistical offices in CEECs would need to abandon or curtail some existing statistical programmes. Statistical offices in OECD countries have often found this difficult to do.

Role of international organisations

The Conference next considered what part the international organisations could play. Formal training for government statisticians is offered by several institutions. The International Monetary Fund gives eight-week courses at its headquarters on balance of payments, banking and government finance statistics, and it also organises shorter courses on these topics in regional centres. The United States Government provides a wide range of courses through its various statistical bureaus – chiefly the Bureau of Economic Analysis, the Bureau of Labour Statistics and the Census Bureau.

Aside from formal training programmes, participants put great value on the informal training that comes through participation in international statistical working groups. The OECD has ten regular working groups that meet to discuss a wide range of statistical questions. In addition to strictly economic statistics they also deal with statistics on environment, energy, agriculture and science. Statisticians from the CEECs could participate in many of these groups even without being members of OECD.

The OECD Secretariat has also produced manuals on a variety of statistical issues. For example, it has published several reports on national accounting including the measurement of profits, real value added, subsistence activities, inflation accounting and the measurement of service output. Reports have also been published on the methods and sources of basic data used by its Member countries for compiling consumer price indices, monetary and financial statistics, cyclical and leading indicators, industrial output and business surveys. Many of these technical manuals would be of use to statisticians from CEECs and, in considering future work in this area, the Secretariat would particularly bear in mind the needs of statistical offices in CEECs.

In closing the Conference, the Secretariat emphasised that its statistical activities are closely linked to policy needs. The OECD's statistical publications, working groups and methodological reports are designed to support policy-oriented analytic work. The Secretariat will use the results of this Conference to design assistance projects in statistics for the CEECs. These projects may cover statistics on labour markets, science and technology, government finance, agriculture, environment and energy as well as economic statistics, but their common feature will be their direct link with policy requirements.

II

Data Needs for Policy Purposes

Statistical Needs of the Solidarity Trade Union: the Polish Experience

Krzysztof Hagemejer
Solidarity, Poland

From its earliest days, the Solidarity Trade Union has stressed the need for impartial statistics on the economic and social situation in Poland. In the decade since 1980 there has been substantial, albeit uneven, progress in developing a more open and credible statistical system in Poland subject to scrutiny by representatives of trade unions, government and scientific institutions. The paper comments critically on the quality and coverage of the statistics needed by the trade unions in Poland – notably statistics on consumer prices, wages, incomes, employment, unemployment and working conditions.

I. Introduction

Every trade union needs statistical information of various kinds to perform its statutory responsibilities – starting with statistics on its membership, then moving to information about wages, incomes, costs of living, labour market, conditions of work and ending with data about the global economic situation of the country.

Only rarely – and only with regard to certain areas – do trade unions have their own sources of statistical data. In the majority of cases they must use data provided by specialised institutions – primarily by national statistical offices. In this situation it is very important to ensure the credibility of official data by means of various forms of control over the national statistical system. Because of the specific needs of trade unions, it is also necessary for them to have close cooperation with the national statistical office and for trade unions to have an influence on the scope and methods of statistical investigations.

II. The Polish experience in the eighties

In the past, all access to statistical information was under state control in Poland – as indeed was the case in other Central and Eastern European countries (CEECs). The authorities used statistics as a tool of propaganda, hiding information about the real economic situation of the country. In addition, because the system of collecting statistical data was connected with reporting on the realisation of the Central Plan, falsification and manipulation of data occurred at all levels in the hierarchy of the economic administration. This resulted in widespread distrust of official statistical information.

The Solidarity Trade Union recognised, from the moment of its origin, that the reform of the state statistical system was a matter of the greatest importance. One of the aims of the August 1980 strikes was to give "the public full information about the social and economic situation..." and in the Gdansk Agreement it was written:

> "Only an aware society, well informed about reality, will be able to initiate and implement a programme for putting our economy in order. The government will radically increase the range of social and economic information available to the public, to trade unions and to economic and social organisations." (*The Birth of Solidarity. The Gdansk Negotiations, 1980*, MacMillan Press, 1983.)

The Gdansk and Szczecin Agreements of 1980 also took up specific questions of statistical information, primarily those concerning prices and the cost of living. The government pledged to improve its methods of investigating price movements and changes in the cost of living and to create conditions for public control of investigations carried out by the Central Statistical Office. Independent investigations of the cost of living and, more generally, of living conditions were also provided for. It also pledged to start work on establishing a so-called "social minimum" – i.e. a level of income which would guarantee a minimum level of consumption expenditures considered as socially indispensable. This was to be used in social policy for fixing the "poverty line" and for calculating minimum wages, pensions and other social benefits.

The years 1980 and 1981 really brought very important changes to the Polish statistical system. The range of information available to the public increased and the trade unions obtained a broader access to statistical data. An informal system of cooperation between trade unions and the state statistical office emerged and the quality of statistical information on price movements, household incomes and expenditures, conditions of work, etc., improved.

But the political situation in this period and, in particular, the later imposition of martial law and the delegalisation of Solidarity were not conducive to an increase in the general credibility of official statistics. Though positive changes introduced earlier were not withdrawn, one can say that during the period 1982-1988 the process of reforming the statistical system in Poland was noticeably slowed down. And though there is no doubt that the quality of Polish official statistics compared very well with the majority of other CEECs at this time, many restrictions on access to data were still retained, statistical information concerning living standards and working conditions were still questionable in many aspects and the scale of public control was very limited. So was public confidence in official statistical information.

During the period of growing inflation, intense shortages, and falling real wages and other incomes, Solidarity, acting illegally, stood up continuously for the interests of the imperilled workers and for a deep reform of the economic system. Various reports on the economic and social situation were prepared by Solidarity; they were based mainly on official data – but after careful analysis and verification. Estimates published by various international organisations also proved very helpful. At this time underground bodies of Solidarity took the unprecedented step of carrying out independent surveys of the cost of living. During 1984 a survey of workers' households was conducted and from then until 1989 consumer prices were surveyed each quarter. Of course, these investigations were on a narrow scale and the results were not fully representative, but independently calculated consumer price indices were a kind of trump card for Solidarity and at least allowed some control and verification of the official data.

The problems of open public access to statistical information and of the need for institutionalised public control over the state statistical system was among the most important subjects of the "Round Table" talks between Solidarity and the government in 1989. As a result of the "Round Table" agreement and of the further political changes in Poland during 1989 and 1990, significant changes took place in the statistical system. They consisted of radical cuts in the list of restricted statistical information and of submitting the state statistical system to public inspection. The Consultation Council was created at the Central Statistical Office. It has the right to present opinions on all aspects of the statistical system, including its organisation, research programme, methods used, forms and scope of publications, etc. The opinions of the Council are of a binding character on the Central Statistical Office, at least as far as consumer price statistics and environmental statistics are concerned. The Council consists of representatives of trade unions and organisations representing other interests and representatives of government, scientific societies and institutions.

III. Basic economic and social data needs of trade unions in the transition period

The new situation does not mean that the many problems existing in the past have been instantly solved. Moreover, the process of transforming all aspects of life in the country generates a lot of new problems which have to be solved. The Polish statistical system, which was created to fulfil the needs of a state-owned, centrally-planned economy, is now facing deep changes that are necessary to adapt it to the needs of a market economy with a growing private sector. The present stabilisation programme and the introduction of market mechanisms are unavoidably tied up with serious social costs, with far-reaching changes in living conditions and with changes in income distribution. The present statistical system is not fully able to generate all the information necessary to properly analyse the social and economic changes that are taking place in Poland. The following paragraphs describe some of the key problems which need an urgent solution, especially from the point of view of the trade unions.

Consumer price indices

Although considerable progress has been made in this domain there is still much to be done to have an exact picture of the consequences of price movements. Up to now, price indices were strongly biased because of intense market shortages and of an administered pricing system. In this situation a commodity chosen as "representative" was very often simply not available on the market and its price movements might be uncorrelated with the price changes of other commodities in the same, even quite narrow, commodity group. Less intense shortages and even excess supply on some markets, which have been features of the Polish economy since the stabilisation programme was introduced, will probably make it easier to estimate price movements.

However, tremendous imperfections in markets still make it very difficult to choose truly representative commodities.

At present, two kinds of consumer price indices are calculated. For the first one, the Retail Price Index of Consumer Goods and Services, estimated values of retail sales are used as weights. The second one, Cost of Living Index, is weighted with consumer expenditures estimated from household budget surveys. It is calculated for four types of households: non-agricultural employees, peasants, pensioners and people employed outside agriculture but also working on their own farms.

The main problem with both weighting systems is the present classification of consumer expenditures. Within the same group of expenditures, goods differ radically from the point of view of their use values, their quality and their price levels. In the same group one can find both goods bought to fulfil basic needs and those bought as luxuries. This system of classification makes it very difficult to evaluate the impact of price movements for changes in the cost of living of people with different levels of incomes. A new classification should be constructed which will be based as closely as possible on product groups defined in terms of consumer needs.

Because of the sharp changes in the pattern of expenditure now taking place in Poland due to falling real income and changing relative prices, the present method of using consumption patterns from the previous year as weights is inadequate. For example, monthly price indices for 1990 are calculated using the 1989 average consumption pattern as the weighting system. (For the first months of 1990 the 1988 consumption pattern was used.) Because at the same time there was a sharp rise in the share of food and some basic consumer services in the consumer expenditures, this method caused price indices to be severely biased and, probably, to underestimate price increases.

The privatisation process, especially visible in retail trade, is also, up to now, not reflected in price index calculations. The share of goods and services bought from private sources is underestimated and the system of price collection leaves out many private trade establishments.

The calculation of price indices is not fully adapted to the new situation in which there are regional differences in price levels and price movements. There is not enough information to take account of regional price differences in calculating the average price index for the whole country.

Apart from credible information about average (national) consumer price movements, it is also very important for a trade union to have at its disposal the whole set of consumer price indices calculated for particular regions of the country, for large agglomerations and small towns, for particular social and professional groups, for households with different income levels and for households of various kinds according to profession, size, age, etc. The present statistical system is unable to generate such information which is, however, necessary to evaluate properly the social changes going on within the country.

Wages and incomes

Considering the steep fall in real wages that has been occurring since the second half of 1989, it is very important to have fast and reliable statistical information concerning the wage levels and wage movements both in the whole economy and in the different sectors, professions and regions. It is also of great importance to have data making it possible to assess changes in patterns of wage differentials. Because of the continuing inflation (though on a lesser scale than a few months ago) all these data should be available monthly or at least quarterly, and with the shortest delay possible.

Up to now, the available data on wages do not permit short-term changes in the wage situation to be assessed. Monthly data on average wage levels are only available for state-owned industries and for some other branches of the state sector. Data on other wages within the state sector (i.e. for about 50 per cent of all the employees) are only available quarterly or even half-yearly and there is a complete lack of information about wages in the private sector. Monthly data on wages published by the Central Statistical Office are not seasonally-adjusted (the same applies also to nearly all monthly data published, e.g. on output, prices, etc.) and this makes it very difficult to evaluate short-term changes in the economy.

Not only are more exact data urgently needed on the wage situation, but it is also equally important to have a full picture of other income changes and of the income situation of different types of households. Household budget surveys, which are the main source of information on income differentials, leave out many social groups – notably those with the highest and lowest incomes. Hitherto, the households of the self-employed and of those working in the private non-agricultural sectors have been excluded from the surveys. Of course there are many obstacles that cannot be quickly eliminated. One can mention here the reluctance of many persons to participate in such surveys, the substantial incomes earned in the "second economy" and as such very seldom reported in surveys, and the lack of a personal income tax system which could provide data to cross-check household survey results.

Apart from all these difficulties it is of great importance to have at the disposal of policy-makers and trade unions the fullest possible information on income differentials and changes in the living conditions of different types of families. On the basis of the information presently available it is nearly impossible to estimate the real social consequences of the present economic changes in Poland, and so it is very difficult to elaborate an appropriate social policy.

Labour market and unemployment

Unemployment – excess supply on the labour market – is a new economic and social phenomenon in the history of post-war Poland. At the same time it is a phenomenon whose uncontrolled social consequences can be a substantial threat to the reforms adopted in Poland and other CEECs. This is why the trade unions pay special attention to activities aimed at minimising the magnitude of unemployment, so that it does not exceed the proportion that is genuinely unavoidable in the process of transition and so that it does not become a long-lasting and mass phenomenon. The present statistical system is not yet prepared to generate credible data on the extent of unemployment in the country as a whole and by regions, nor on its nature and causes. There is a strong need for intensive statistical surveys of unemployment covering age patterns, levels of education, professional qualifications, living conditions, etc.

Working conditions

The data presently available on hours of work and *working conditions* – e.g. number of employed working in dangerous or health-affecting conditions or the number of accidents at work – are limited only to the state sector of the economy. The development of the private sector that is expected in Poland in the near future should not cause a deterioration in the working conditions of employees; there are many examples to show that this danger does exist. Therefore collection of data on working conditions from the private sector as well is urgent and necessary.

IV. Conclusions

Solidarity itself is collecting statistical data, with the help of its own research centres, on the most important present social problems. Surveys are conducted in various areas – unemployment, working conditions, economic condition of enterprises, wage situation of employees, living conditions of families. The results obtained allow us – at least partially – to fill some gaps existing in the national statistical system and they are very useful for shaping trade union policy. But financial and technical possibilities are too limited to conduct a research programme on the scale needed. And of course such trade union statistical investigations will never be a substitute for investigations by the national statistical office. That is why Solidarity insists on rapid changes to the national statistical system.

This note has mentioned only some of the most important problems that must be solved to get data that will allow us to estimate and analyse the rapid changes now occurring in the economic and social situation in Poland. These data would allow trade unions to achieve their statutory aims and, at the same time, to participate in the transition of the economic system from a centrally-planned to a market system – a transition that is necessary but may bring great hardship to the population. These problems are probably not confined to Poland but apply to many other countries that are taking the same or a similar route. In addition to the efforts of the state and of the trade unions to solve these problems, there is, in the author's view, need for various forms of external help from foreign governments, from trade unions and from international organisations.

Data Needs of Trade Unions: Towards a Common Framework

David Lea

Trades Union Congress, United Kingdom

This note draws on experience at national and international levels to identify the data needs of the trade unions in their role as social partners. These needs go beyond conventional bargaining statistics such as prices and earnings and include statistics on profitability, labour productivity, "social wages" and international competitiveness. The paper also considers the conditions for creating and maintaining the credibility of official statistics. It argues that responsibility should be centralised in an agency whose independence is guaranteed by law. The work of this agency should be periodically reviewed by a consultative committee which includes representatives from the trade unions, business and the universities.

I. Introduction

In the countries of Central and Eastern Europe there are fundamental differences from the accounting conventions used in the market-based economies of the OECD. As the economies of Central and Eastern Europe shift towards more market-based systems, this will demand new statistical measures. This note is intended to assist the debate on how this might be handled, drawing on the experiences of the UK trade union movement at both the national and international level, through bodies such as Eurostat, the European Commission and the OECD.

The long-term aim for the 1990s from such a dialogue could be the creation of a common framework for statistical information, reflecting both the situation in OECD industrialised countries and the evolution of Central and Eastern European economies towards more market-based economies. Nor should it be assumed that the debate will be all one way – there may be valuable lessons from the experiences of Central and Eastern European trade unions which could be used to develop and improve the statistics of the OECD.

II. Data needs of trade unions

Trade union role

Trade unions are major users of information, not only for collective bargaining purposes but also in their wider role as social partners. This is explicitly recognised in

ILO Convention 160 (the Labour Statistics Convention) adopted in 1985. Under Article 3 of the Convention it says:

> "In designing or revising the concepts, definitions, and methodology used in the collection, compilation and publication of the statistics required under this Convention, the representative organisations of employers and workers, where they exist, shall be consulted with a view to taking into account their needs and to ensuring their cooperation".

Trade unions believe that consultation and participation is not only crucial to retrieving the credibility of official statistics, it will result in better statistics, and hence more informed decisions by Government, employers, and trade unions.

Collective bargaining and the labour market

Trade unions are major users of statistics for collective bargaining purposes, especially statistics relating to prices and earnings. Experience suggests that for wage bargainers, the cost of living is one of the single most important factors in influencing the level of pay settlements – although other considerations, such as profitability, comparability with similar groups of workers, and productivity improvements are also important. However, trade unions are not simply passive recipients. Trade unions were one of the first suppliers of unemployment figures, and today the experiences of union officers have helped develop statistical measures which, as far as possible, provide an accurate and up to date picture. The role of trade unions in drawing up statistics on earnings, prices and employment statistics is described below by way of illustrating these points. The wider need in Central and Eastern Europe is to develop statistics as part of the introduction of an active labour market policy.

International comparisons

The scale of collective bargaining is moving from the national to the international level across a number of industrial sectors. Multinational companies frequently inform their own approach to collective bargaining and future investment plans by making comparisons between different plants using measures of productivity and profitability. Trade unions are equally concerned with these and other bases for comparison, such as earnings and hours worked. Unions in low wage economies will clearly be concerned that economic progress and restructuring allows – over time – for real wage levels and conditions to move up to the best. Unions in high wage economies will be equally concerned that their terms and conditions are not undermined in competition with low wage economies. Upward harmonisation of pay and conditions will act as a spur to improve competitive performance, but the starting point in all these areas is for detailed information on the make-up of labour markets in industrialised countries both in the European Community and outside, including pay, conditions, productivity, investment levels, training, and research and development. The European Trade Union Confederation (ETUC) is discussing these issues, and the European Trade Union Institute (ETUI) publishes an annual report on collective bargaining developments in Western Europe. Further details of trade union work is set out in the TUC report, *Europe 1992: Progress Report on Trade Union Objectives*.

Inward investment

The need for accurate, internationally comparable information is important in regard to inward investment. The official labour cost statistics produced by the OECD, the ILO, and the European Commission could be misused to exert pressures on wages and wage costs. In 1982, a working party of the European Trade Union Confederation (ETUC) set out a number of concerns at the way cost statistics were being drawn up, and called for:

i) Faster production of up to date figures
ii) Coverage to extend to all enterprises and all workers
iii) Restricted definition of "labour costs" to exclude items such as training and taxes
iv) Access by trade unions at the enterprise or workplace level to information supplied by employers to ensure its accuracy.

It is worth noting, however, that the evidence suggests that labour costs per se are not the major influence on the majority of inward investment decisions in the industrialised countries. Table 1 below shows that it is market-related reasons which are overwhelmingly important, as well as the need to integrate with existing investment. However, growing importance is being given to adequately trained and skilled workers able to operate efficiently the technically-advanced equipment on which the firms' competitive edge depends. This may mean that statistics on training and retraining will assume greater importance when inward investors come to make comparisons between countries.

Table 1. **Main influences on foreign direct investment decisions in industrialised countries**

Reason	Percentage of Respondents 1970	1983
Access to host domestic market	89	67
Access to host regional market	41	37
Avoid tariff trade barriers	24	16
Avoid non-tariff trade barriers	13	8
Integrate with existing investment	26	37
Change in industrial structure	20	22
Slow growth at home	17	18
Access to raw materials	13	10
Inducements by host country	11	12
Integrate other companies investment	4	8
Comparative labour costs	4	6

Notes: Figures are per cent of respondents mentioning a factor in their "top three".Other factors put to respondents were comparative material costs, shifts in political and social stability, tax advantages, market presence, distribution of risk, return on R&D, development of local market, acquisition opportunities, exchange rate shifts.
Source: Group of Thirty, Foreign Direct Investment, 1973-87.

Trade unions as social partners

Trade unions have a wider interest apart from statistics of direct use in collective bargaining. Statistics on the macro-economy such as output, investment, and trade are important to trade unions in their roles as social partners. Where trade union cooperation and participation is being sought in economic and industrial policy, the basis for agreement must rest on agreed measures of how fast the economy is growing, the rate of expansion of industrial output, and the relative strengths of exports and imports. This has been the approach adopted in the TUC's call for a National Economic Assessment in the United Kingdom. It is also vital in efforts to promote stronger economic policy cooperation at the international level, as called for by the OECD and the European Commission.

Trade unions in the wider context are also interested in the "social wage", the level and distribution of social benefits which have a rôle to play in establishing national consensus on wage levels. In the past, understandings have commonly been reached between employers, trade unions, and government on how moderation of wage increases might be offset by improvements in the social wage. Within the context of European integration, the importance of such measures will become more important in the 1990s. The very large differences that exist between European Community (EC) members in terms of social protection benefits per head will need to be brought into harmony, over time, by a process of levelling up to the more efficient economies in the EC. This convergence reflects the importance trade unions attach to the social dimension of European integration, just as much as the importance given to converging inflation rates in the interest of monetary union, and the reduction of regional inequalities in the interests of economic integration. This is recognised by international statistical bodies such as Eurostat which is currently trying to improve statistical coverage in areas such as education, training, health and safety, poverty and the environment to complement existing labour market indicators. The importance of these "new agenda" indicators should be recognised.

Industrial competitiveness

A similar wider concern is when more detailed statistics are collected on a sector-by-sector basis. These not only provide information to Government, they are a vital measure for firms and trade unions about how well their industry is performing, and how well the individual company is doing relative to the rest of industry. It is important to see industrial level statistics not primarily as a burden imposed by government on industry, but as a vital competitive tool. Recently the knitting industry sector group of the National Economic Development Council has asked for the reinstatement of official statistics because the lack of information was placing the sector at a disadvantage vis-à-vis foreign competitors.

III. Towards credible statistics

Independence and credibility

Statistical information must be produced independently from government and political pressure, and the measure adopted must have widespread acceptance by the major users of statistics if it is to achieve credibility. Once it is believed that government is manipulating information for short-term political gain or to obscure the underlying situation, then credibility is rapidly lost. Even when subsequent information is accurately presented, it will tend not to be believed. This in turn can lead to a proliferation of "unofficial" estimates and indices, each reflecting the particular interests of the parties concerned. Under such circumstances, policy debate can become a sterile exchange of statistical numbers while the major underlying policy issues are neglected.

The loss of credibility not only impacts on non-governmental users of statistics, but can also lead to loss of confidence within government in its own statistics. Once Government Ministries or Departments decide the official statistics are providing a misleading picture, the pursuit of policy objectives is unlikely to proceed in an efficient or effective manner. The chances of inappropriate or mistaken policy objectives being adopted will also be increased. This may be more likely to happen if statistical information is decentralised: until recently, in the United Kingdom each major Ministry was responsible for statistics on its particular policy area. Not only is the possibility of discrepancies between statistical series increased, but the suspicion is raised that the information reflects the concerns of particular Ministries and not the wider needs of government and the major users of statistics.

It is not enough that statistical information is in reality free from political interference, it must also be seen to be so. There are many good technical reasons why the basis for statistical indices must be changed from time to time, and statisticians are always eager to improve the accuracy of the information they provide. The reasons for change are not always easily understood or communicated to the general public, and it is easy for a technical change to be mis-represented as political manipulation. To guard against such suspicions, justified or not, the oversight of statistical information must be distanced from Government. The development of independent bureaux – such as the United States Bureau of Labor Statistics (BLS) – has been an important safeguard, but equally important is the active participation of statistical users – the academic community, industry and trade unions – in developing methodologies for calculation and advising on technical change and development.

In the United Kingdom, oversight by independent tripartite advisory committees of key statistical indicators has been urged by the TUC and others. A recent report from the Royal Statistical Society (RSS) makes clear that while the integrity of government officials is undoubted, there are major concerns that statisticians are coming under undue pressure from politicians and that public confidence in the independence of statistics has been undermined. The RSS is calling for the collection of statistics to be centralised fully under the Central Statistical Office; for a Statistics Act; and for a National Statistics Commission. The TUC, in a Memorandum to the Government in 1981, had previously called for a National Statistical Council to involve all statistical representatives.

Statistics as a public good

The provision of credible statistics can only be realistically carried out by government (or a public agency) which publishes information which is free and accessible to all interested parties. Statistics produced by a private organisation – whether profit making or not – will be treated with suspicion. Government alone is in a position to compel the provision of statistics, apply consistency of definition, and work with international bodies. The provision of statistical information by profit-making organisations obviously restricts the availability of statistics to those who can afford to pay. Similarly, user charges (a policy adopted by the United Kingdom Government) for some statistical information will tend to see wealthier interests in society gain privileged access to public information. More fundamentally, the public provision of statistical information which is free and accessible to all – irrespective of position or wealth – can make an important contribution to the development and strengthening of more democratic forms of government, inform open and public debate of the major issues, and encourage the active participation of different interest groups within society in the democratic process.

International statistical agencies

The development of a wide range of comparators on productivity and unit labour costs, on the social wage, on unemployment and on vacancies underlines the key role of international agencies such as Eurostat, the OECD and the ILO in providing acceptable common definitions. These are not always easy to reach agreement on, reflecting differences in institutional arrangements, demographic factors and so on. There are also major differences in national assumptions – for example, some countries assume productivity growth in the public sector is 1 per cent, others 2 per cent, others 0 per cent. Eurostat is trying to deepen its contacts with Central Banks to get information on financial movements – these are particularly relevant to the operations of multinational companies. However, it is a matter of concern to the ETUC and the TUC that a project to build data bases on multinational companies has had to be shelved because of lack of political support. Eurostat and other international agencies are facing immense problems because of their dependence on national statistical information, which has faced both public expenditure cuts and the resistance of firms to provide the necessary facts and figures.

IV. Trade union experience in the United Kingdom

Trade unions in the United Kingdom, as elsewhere, are major users of a wide range of economic and social statistics. In the United Kingdom trade unions have had a more direct role and concern in four main areas: earnings, prices, employment and unemployment – and the labour market more generally, including redundancy and structural change – and industrial output and production.

Earnings

The official survey of earnings in the United Kingdom – the New Earnings Survey – was initially overseen in 1968 by a small technical working party of government officials and statisticians, employers and the TUC. The working party's remit was to look at the preliminary results, consider how they might be published and the implications for other government surveys. The TUC, as a major user of the statistics, is consulted on a regular basis.

Prices

In Britain, the standard measure of inflation is the Retail Prices Index (RPI). The Retail Prices Index Advisory Committee (RPIAC) is convened from time to time by the Minister responsible for the RPI (formerly the Secretary of State for Employment and now the Chancellor of the Exchequer) and makes recommendations on the method of construction and compilation of the index. The advisory Committee comprises representatives from a wide range of interest groups – the Government, the Central Bank, the Civil Service, the Trades Union Congress, the Confederation of British Industry (the employers representative body in the United Kingdom), academia and the voluntary sector. As such its views are generally accepted to be consensual and non partisan. The nature and composition of the RPIAC has meant that the index itself – and the inflation figure it represents – is seen as having considerable credibility by all parties. A unilateral attempt in the early 1980s to introduce a new index (the tax and price index) by the Government failed to win support, and is largely ignored by policy-makers and wage-bargainers.

Until inflation started to rise again in the United Kingdom in recent years, the RPI had appeared to be immune from the sort of criticisms and alterations that other sets of centrally-produced statistics have been subject to. However, increases in interest rates – designed to contain inflationary pressures – began to feed through to the housing costs element of the index. There followed some suggestions from both inside and outside government circles that the index itself was at fault; Government members began to talk in terms of an "underlying" rate of inflation excluding mortgage costs – and later also the "poll tax" (a new system of raising local authority finance introduced by the Government as a flat rate charge for locally-provided services). The recommendations of the RPIAC was that – despite some technical difficulties and having regard to the special role of mortgage payments in the United Kingdom housing market – the inclusion of both these indicators was legitimate and enhanced the accuracy of the index as a reflection of the cost of living.

There have been efforts by some commentators to promote an "alternative" index which excluded mortgage payments and attempted to take into account capital appreciation in house values. It also left out the poll tax. The RPIAC itself had considered this problem in 1986 and had concluded that "though there is a case in principle for taking account of the capital appreciation of mortgaged housing in assessing owner occupiers' costs, there is no satisfactory method of doing so". In 1989 the RPIAC also undertook a detailed consideration of the case for including the "Community Charge" in the RPI. It may be seen as a tax on residence in a particular local authority area or as a payment for services.

The dangers of producing ad hoc alternative "indices" are clear. The official RPI is well understood by the British public. Such attempts to undermine its credibility can only cause confusion and may in turn lead to a proliferation of alternative indices. For this reason the TUC itself accepted the RPIAC recommendation, made in 1986, that it would not be advisable to publish a separate index for low-paid workers – clearly negotiators at many levels would be able to argue for whichever indicator suited their particular purpose. Indeed more recently the Government itself has appeared to be increasingly concerned to deter attempts to undermine the RPI. A recent press release from the Central Statistical Office stated that "special indices may be seen as additions to the general RPI, which are useful for analytical purposes, but none of them is presented as an *alternative* to the official view or to the official index or would be acceptable as an immediate replacement for it".

Employment and unemployment

The Government instituted a number of cut-backs in the coverage of the employment statistics from 1981 onwards. The result has been considerable revisions of the employment figures from year to year. This has also caused major changes to other important variables, such as productivity. The TUC has frequently criticised these short-comings, and earlier this year the Government announced the restoration of an annual Census of Employment, and further improvements to the household-based Labour Force Survey.

The high levels of unemployment seen in OECD industrial countries in the 1980s have been accompanied by supply side measures, including training, early retirement and similar schemes. This has created difficulties of classification between the unemployed, employed and trainees and those counted as in the labour force and those counted as being outside the labour force. ILO recommendations on these problems have now been agreed, but in Britain the ILO recommendations are not followed consistently within Government.

In all OECD countries the government maintains an employment service, at which those who seek work or new jobs can "register" their interest, and from which employers with vacancies seek referrals. These have many advantages, but the fact that administrative data depend on the administrative regulation in force may tend to invalidate not only international comparisons but also comparisons between groups of the population. A noticeable feature of the labour market in the United Kingdom, for example, is the relatively low rate of female unemployment according to the official count compared to any other European Community country. This at least in part reflects the benefit entitlement and thus how many would be registered as unemployed. Eurostat figures suggest female unemployment is under-estimated in the United Kingdom by 40 per cent. This also has implications for the sort of employment services which should be offered to the unemployed: the United Kingdom may be under-investing in services adapted to the needs of unemployed women.

In the United Kingdom, there have been 27 changes since 1978 to the method by which the official unemployment count is calculated. The TUC has always accepted that changes in the ways statistics are compiled have to reflect new forms of employment and other developments in the labour market. However, the lack of an established and well-respected tripartite advisory body, such as the one that exists for the RPI, means that such changes have undermined public confidence in the unemployment figures. The TUC – as have from time to time the employers organisations – has frequently called upon the United Kingdom Government to set up an independent tripartite advisory committee to oversee the production of labour market statistics.

Production statistics

The TUC is represented on the Production Industry Statistics Advisory Committee, but the attitude of the United Kingdom Government is summed up in the 1988 official review of statistics produced by the Department of Trade and Industry which stated: "we have not given much consideration to users outside government". The review resulted in a dramatic cut-back in production statistics. In 1990 Sir Douglas Wass, previously Treasury Permanent Secretary, commented that statistics in Britain are inferior "to those in nearly all our competitor countries". The Chairman of the Statistics Users' Council said it was no longer possible to determine in detail import penetration, export performance, productivity, market share, and United Kingdom home demand across a range of industries. There is now recognition by the United Kingdom Government that the cuts went too far, and improvements are being sought.

V. Conclusions

The following points summarise the main recommendations and concerns of the TUC, drawing on experience both at the national and international level. It is hoped that these will be of assistance to Central and Eastern European countries in developing and improving their national statistical sources, and to ensure better comparability between OECD countries and Central and Eastern European economies.

i) Legitimacy and confidence in national and international statistics are essential. This will require:

- *a)* Centralisation of responsibility for statistical information;
- *b)* Creation of independent statistical bureaux with statutory backing;
- *c)* Guaranteed resources to meet quality standards for existing statistics and to develop new indices.

ii) Consultation with trade unions and other social partners, including the academic community. This should include:

- *a)* Independent, tripartite advisory committees to oversee key statistics;
- *b)* Consultation by National Bureaux with trade unions as required under ILO Convention 160;
- *c)* Unions at the enterprise or workplace level to have access to information supplied by firms to official surveys to ensure accuracy;
- *d)* Regular consultative meetings between international bureaux and–appropriate trade union bodies.

iii) New indices should be developed to reflect wider concerns, especially in regard to the "social dimension". These might include:

- *a)* A "hardship index" combining data on low pay and other labour market indicators;
- *b)* Indicators on training and skill levels;

c) Environmental indicators – related to guidelines to environmental audits by enterprises called for by the UN ECE Conference in Bergen, Norway, in May 1990 which agreed that in preparing Environment Audits firms should consult workers and their trade union representatives; and

d) Databases on multinational companies.

iv) Information on existing labour market areas should be improved and strengthened; in particular measures of labour costs should not be widened so as to give misleading impressions.

v) International comparability should be encouraged; some OECD countries are way behind others in terms of quality and coverage of statistical information.

vi) International statistical agencies, including Eurostat, OECD and ILO should be strengthened and supported.

It is particularly important that the inevitable changes in relative prices, and possible overall rise in prices, are accurately and credibly reflected in the process of economic change now taking place in Central and Eastern Europe. Likewise, hitherto exclusively Western phenomena such as redundancy and related structural change require an urgent labour market statistical context, so that the necessary debate on policy options – and indeed responses by employers and unions – can distinguish between the issue of how far a price change is taking place and how far it is correct for unions to try and compensate for this against the background of an economy in transition.

Economic Statistics Used by the Business Sector

Business and Industry Advisory Committee and
Economics and Statistics Department, OECD

The Business and Industry Advisory Committee to the OECD surveyed its members to find out what kinds of economic statistics are used most often by industrial and commercial organisations in OECD countries. The purpose was to identify subject areas that statistical offices in Central and Eastern European countries should pay particular attention to as they move to market economies. The survey showed that the OECD business sector attaches high priority to statistics on wages, foreign transactions, domestic finance, labour force, production, national accounts and prices. For most purposes highly aggregated data are needed.

I. Introduction

For private enterprises, economic analysis is valuable not only for making financial forecasts to determine the profitability of a potential new investment, but also for making effective strategic planning decisions for existing operations.

Which statistics are considered most useful by the business sector for assessing national economic conditions? To answer this question, the Business and Industry Advisory Committee to the OECD (BIAC) surveyed its Economic Policy Committee (EPC) using a questionnaire prepared by the OECD Economics and Statistics Department. The 18 respondents were representative of the BIAC EPC membership, which is comprised of business economists from multinational enterprises, international banks, and national industry and employer federations from the 24 OECD Member countries.

II. Results

The questionnaire listed 80 economic statistics grouped into 15 subjects areas. The 80 series were taken from the various statistical publications of the Economic and Statistics Department and are representative of the economic statistics commonly published in OECD Member countries. Respondents were asked to indicate whether each series listed in the questionnaire is regarded as "highly important", "less important" or "is rarely or never used". Table 1 shows the percentage of respondent who assigned these various priorities to series within each of the 15 subject areas.

Table 1. **Percent of respondents reporting use of different types of economic statistics**

Subject area	Highly used	Less used	Rarely used
National accounts	68	26	6
Production	71	20	9
Cyclical indicators	53	47	0
Business surveys	59	31	10
Deliveries, sales, stocks and orders	38	34	28
Construction	37	31	32
Domestic trade	45	36	19
Labour	73	19	8
Wages	94	6	0
Prices	69	23	8
Domestic finance	71	29	0
Interest rates, share prices	74	23	3
Foreign finance	68	22	10
Foreign trade	85	10	5
Balance of payments	81	19	0
All subject areas	64	25	11

Note: The percentages are averaged over the priorities assigned to the various series identified under each subject area.

Nearly two-thirds of respondents (64 per cent) assigned high priority to all the economic statistics listed in the questionnaire and only 11 per cent, on average, reported that they were rarely or never used. This is no small encouragement to statisticians in OECD countries. What they are producing is generally seen as useful by the business sector.

Over 80 per cent of respondents reported "wages", "foreign trade" and "balance of payments" statistics as highly used while, at the other end of the scale, about 20 per cent or more reported that data on "construction", "deliveries, sales, stocks and orders" and "domestic trade" are rarely or never used. In Table 2 the subject areas have been ranked by assigning weights of 2, 1 and 0, respectively, to the percentages under "highly used", "less used" and "rarely used". The table may be taken as broadly indicative of the importance attached by the business sector in OECD countries to these 15 types of economic statistics, although it should be emphasised that the rankings are to some extent determined by the particular series used in the questionnaire to represent each subject area.

Table 3 lists the twenty "most-used statistics". They have been ranked using the same (simple and arbitrary) weighting system as for Table 2. The first five listed in Table 3 are key indicators of domestic economic activity – unit labour costs (i.e. the labour cost or "price" of a unit of real product), total GDP, consumer prices, industrial output and employment. It is interesting to see that the next seven most-used statistics include six foreign sector statistics – exports, imports, terms of trade, current

Table 2. **Economic statistics used by business sector: subject areas ranked by frequency of use**

Rank*	Subject area
1	Wages
2	Balance of payments
3	Foreign trade
4	Domestic finance
5	Interest rates and share prices
6	Labour
7	Production
8	National accounts
9	Prices
10	Foreign finance
11	Cyclical indicators
12	Business surveys
13	Domestic trade
14	Deliveries, sales, stocks and orders
15	Construction

* The ranks are obtained from the percentages given in Table 1 using weights of 2, 1 and 0 for "highly used", "less used" and "rarely used" respectively.

account balance, etc. This reflects the importance of foreign trade in the economies of OECD countries.

A striking – perhaps expected – feature of the 20 series in Table 3 is that they are virtually all total (i.e. whole-economy) statistics. The overall consumer price index is a most-used statistic but there is much less interest in its breakdown into food and energy components; the total unemployment rate is a most-used statistic but not the breakdown by sex or age group; total imports and exports appear high in the list but the breakdown of exports by commodities is at the bottom and there is even less interest in partner country detail.

The ranking procedure used for Table 3 was applied to all 80 statistics. It confirmed that detailed breakdowns are, on average, accorded a rather low priority by the business sector. Among the 80 statistics on offer, "stocks by stage of fabrication" and "unfilled orders by kind of industrial activity" aroused the least interest among the 18 respondents.

Popularity polls of the kind described in this note are interesting for both users and producers of statistics, but there are some obvious difficulties in using their results for deciding statistical priorities. First and most obvious, the fact that "total" statistics are seen as more useful than their detailed components has little practical interest. Almost always the totals are obtained by adding up the components: statistical offices cannot, therefore, save money by only compiling the totals.

Table 3. **The twenty most-used statistics**

Name of series	Rank
Unit labour costs	1
Gross Domestic Product, total	1
Retail/Consumer prices, total	1
Industrial production index, total	4
Unemployment, total	4
Exports, total	4
Trade balance	4
Terms of trade	4
Merchandise trade balance	4
GDP by expenditure	4
Exchange rates	11
Imports, total	11
Labour force, total	13
Employment, total	13
Hourly earnings	13
Short-term interest rates	13
Current balance	13
Long-term interest rates	18
GDP by income components	19
Exports by commodities	19

Second, many of the statistics given a low interest rating by the 18 respondents may be very important for them *indirectly*. For example, "business surveys", "cyclical indicators" and "national accounts" all have a relatively low rating as subject areas in themselves. But these statistics are vital ingredients in short-term economic forecast which are of very great interest to the business sector. Again there is not much scope for economising on resources by reducing work in these areas.

III. Other useful national statistics

As part of the survey, BIAC EPC members were asked to identify other national statistics which were not listed on the questionnaire, but which they consider to be useful. These statistics are grouped by the nationality of respondents to this question in Annex 1.

The two principal areas which emerge from this list are public sector financing/spending and technology-related statistics. The latter group includes such items as statistics on intangible investment, and patents, licenses and know-how. Additional areas of interest to more than one of the respondents were regional or sub-national statistics, energy statistics, and statistics on the financial situation of companies. Finally, an interesting point was raised by the German respondent who commented on the growing relevance and usefulness of statistics compiled on the level of regional trading groups relative to those provided at the national level.

Annex 1

Other Useful National Statistics

Austria

Environment statistics (investment, research and development, state of the environment)
Research and development (generally)
Statistics on patents, licenses, and know-how
Fiscal and finance statistics
Foreign/domestic investment statistics
Energy statistics
Transport statistics
Statistics on educational policies

Denmark

Import-export prices
Detailed wage statistics (e.g. industry, sex)

Finland

Technology indicators
Energy consumption
Public finance
Raw material prices

France

Accounts and financial ratios of companies
Statistics on productive supply (stock of capital, time of utilisation of equipment in manufacturing industries)
Intangible investment (research and development, training, etc.)

Germany

Statistics compiled on the level of regional trading groups

Ireland

Trade by category of use (e.g. imports of capital goods, consumer goods)
Migration and population data
Exchequer spending and borrowing – all public sector financing and spending

New Zealand

Public sector finance (basically Treasury accounts for Government Budget, seen as a statistical series)
Local government accounts

Sweden

Public sector revenue and expenditures (total and by category)

United Kingdom

Company liquidity
Regional statistics

Business Investment in Central and Eastern Europe and the Role of Statistical Information

Giorgio Bodo

FIAT S.p.A, Italy

The recent political changes in Europe are opening up new markets in Central and Eastern Europe with great potential benefits to both East and West. Investment by Western companies is hindered by uncertainty both about probable returns to investment and about the current economic situation in these countries. Statistics can play an important role in reducing this uncertainty. In developing their statistics, the Central and Eastern European countries should adopt international standards, aim initially to produce a limited number of basic series rather than large elaborate data systems and publish their statistics on a timely and regular basis.

The recent changes in Central and Eastern Europe have opened new horizons and created possibilities of substantial benefits for business, industry and the world economy. There are big potential gains to be reaped:

- A very large potential market of about the same size as Western Europe (more than 300 hundred million consumers);
- Availability of a labour force, generally well-educated and with a cultural background similar to that of the Western World, at still relatively low costs;
- Possibilities of increasing trade between the two regions, with positive effects on the income and welfare of both areas.

Direct investments are the key to gaining access to these markets, and are also of paramount importance for the development of Central and Eastern Europe. In this way productivity is increased by introducing western management methods and production technology. Investor commitment to future transfers of skills and technology which are critical to the continuing competitiveness of a company in an open market economy, is also assured.

At the same time, however, the risks involved in investing in these regions are very high. The rate of political change has been dramatic but the rate of economic change will necessarily take far more time. Moreover, the problems encountered in the transition from a planned economy to a free market economy are huge. Establishing the principles of a market economy which for us seem to be obvious are not so for people living in countries where communism dominated for more than 40 years. There is a clear lack of entrepreneurial skills, the intensity of work is generally low, there are no financial or monetary markets, there is an urgent need to apply accounting procedures, property rights are not yet always well defined and, in addition, political instabilities have to be faced in certain areas.

It is therefore evident that all the necessary steps to reduce the extent and consequences of these risks should be taken. In this respect statistics can play a very important role. In fact, every time a company plans to enter a certain market it needs data in order to understand the structure of the economy of that particular country and its probable short-term developments. All this is a fundamental part of any short-term evaluation and long-term planning. The usual needs are even more important in the case of Central and Eastern European countries because:

- Knowledge of these economies in the West is very limited;
- The available data are often not comparable to those used in the West (e.g. Net Material Product versus Gross National Product);
- The system of relative prices has been severely distorted and it is therefore extremely difficult to evaluate profitability and economic performance, even in the light of the future changes that will take place with the phasing out of subsidies on most products;
- Although Central and Eastern European countries were all part of the same political bloc, their economies are extremely heterogeneous: the role of the agricultural sector varies to a great extent, there are differences in the importance of the various industrial sectors, etc.

All this leads to a high degree of uncertainty and it makes it much more difficult to define a corporate strategy for Central and Eastern Europe.

For all these reasons, business firms need statistics in order to improve their knowledge of these countries, and they need them with a high degree of urgency with particular reference to basic statistics of national accounts, wages and prices.

Obviously, the task of creating suitable statistics for the new economic system will be a difficult and lengthy process. It will therefore be of extreme importance to establish certain basic criteria:

- Define clear priorities, for not everything can be achieved immediately. Moreover, users should be involved in establishing the priority list right from the beginning;
- Do not try to be overambitious. During the first stage it seems more important to have a certain number of basic statistics in a short period of time, rather than a complete system in the rather distant future;
- Try to stick as far as possible to standard classification schemes in order to achieve comparability within Central and Eastern European countries and vis-à-vis Western European countries. In this field a fundamental role should be played by the international organisations.
- Produce timely statistics. This is an obvious request, but in view of the far-reaching, rapid changes which will take place in these economies it is an important one.
- Try to make all the relevant statistics widely available. Here again, international organisations can be of considerable help by collecting information centrally from Central and Eastern European countries and by disseminating it to all users.

If all this is accomplished, and it is certainly no easy task, then uncertainty will be reduced, so improving our understanding of the characteristics and the workings of Central and Eastern European countries. At the same time this will allow us to evaluate the impact of economic and political reforms. Finally, entrepreneurs will be in a better position to enter into the different markets, thus making a more effective contribution to the development of these regions.

Economic Data Requirements for Short-Term Forecasting in Hungary

Judit Neményi and Andreas Vértes
Economic Research Institute, Hungary

This paper describes how the Economic Research Institute makes its short-term forecasts for the Hungarian economy. These forecasts have made extensive use of data from business surveys and these surveys are expected to become even more important in future because they are the only source available for information on changes in enterprise behaviour as the economy moves to a full market basis. The rapid growth of the private sector is mentioned as a potentially serious problem for data collection. Statistics on the enterprise sector will be incomplete and perhaps misleading unless surveys can be rapidly expanded to cover the full range of producers – state enterprises, privatised companies, joint ventures and small private enterprises.

I. Recent economic developments and prospects

Since 1968, several economic reforms have been introduced in the centrally-directed economy of Hungary, allowing firms partial independence in decision making. As a result, imperfect market mechanisms now coexist with direct control of firms by the central authorities. The economic reforms of the last decades have thus constituted preliminary steps in transforming the centrally-planned economy and the transformation of the political system in Hungary following the elections of May 1990 has created preconditions for fulfilling the double task of economic transformation and stabilisation.

Today, the economy of Hungary is burdened by serious crisis phenomena. Inflation has been accelerating and the inflation rate is expected to exceed 25 per cent in 1990. The effects of monetary rigour have been cancelled by a rapid expansion of trade credit. The Forint 10 billion target budget deficit (a creditworthiness criterion imposed by IMF) has been called into question. The foreign indebtedness, a $20 billion gross convertible debt (i.e. about $2 000 per capita) and increasing debt service obligation, have set nearly impossible requirements for the Hungarian export sector. In order to meet export targets and to solve the chronic current account problems, the Hungarian production structure needs a rapid transformation taking into account world market demand and competitiveness.

Output is overwhelmingly produced by state-owned enterprises. Industrial goods made in Hungary often cannot be sold in the world market or are sold at discounted prices. Because of the introduction of settlements in convertible currencies from

January 1991, trade with COMECON countries is expected to be reduced. In the first half of 1990, the halt to rouble exports which was imposed by the government because of the huge trade surplus with USSR in 1989, resulted in a 30 per cent drop of exports and caused significant production losses as well as employment problems. At the same time, significant growth of non-rouble exports can be observed.

Economic transformation requires that the dominant role of the state should be replaced by an economic system in which free decisions are made primarily by enterprises and individuals and are based on market mechanisms and consumer choice. The reform measures of recent years have created some of the necessary conditions for establishing the main institutions of commodity and capital markets (two tier banking, stock exchange, etc.), but transformation processes have to be accelerated.

A first priority is the transformation of ownership which must be accompanied by measures to encourage both domestic and foreign entrepreneurship. Only rapid privatisation of state-owned firms can improve the productive efficiency of Hungarian industry by reallocating capital to sectors of higher profitability and by encouraging innovations through the pressure of competition. Because of the low level of domestic saving and the underdevelopment of capital market, it will take a long time to sell off all the state-owned enterprises whose book value is estimated at $ 30 billion.

For the successful functioning of a privatised economy, the system of financial regulators (taxation, subsidies, etc.) should be stabilised. The most binding constraint on transformation – the shortage of capital – can be eased by encouraging domestic saving and by assuring favourable financial conditions for both domestic private and foreign direct investments. The liberalisation of prices, wages and convertible imports (actually about 70 per cent of imports are liberalised) should be maintained. Tight monetary and stable fiscal policy should be maintained in order to control inflation. Financial reorganisation of inefficiently producing state-owned firms, which may involve bankruptcy or privatisation, can no longer be postponed.

In the medium term, appropriate transformation policies will permit a switch over from the present stagflation to moderate growth of the Hungarian economy and the convertibility of the Forint.

II. Historical survey of short-term forecasting

Developments in macro-economic forecasting should be briefly surveyed, in order to determine how the above mentioned moves towards a market economy affect data requirements for short-term forecasting in Hungary.

In recent decades, in the centrally-directed economy of Hungary, short-term forecasting and national planning have been closely related. In consequence of economic reforms which gave partial independence to economic agents, policymakers have become interested in policy evaluation and forecasts for purpose of national planning. In a market economy, national planning should focus principally on medium and long-term economic development, being generally well distinguished from both the short run state budgetary policy and business cycle forecasting. In Hungary, however, although medium-term plans have been declared to be the core of the planning activity, the deepening crisis of the 1980s has led to priority being given to annual plans of short run policy decisions. Short-term forecasting has thus become entwined with national planning and with politics. The intensity of the political dependence of short-term forecasting has been decreasing as market mechanisms have been getting stronger.

The National Planning Office (NPO) can be considered as the main centre of short term forecasting in Hungary. Short term forecasts (often dominated by the attitude of the central authorities) have been regularly made by several institutions. Among others, the quarterly revised forecasts made by the Ministry of Finance, the Ministry of Industry and other ministries, and by the National Bank of Hungary should be mentioned. Short term forecasts focusing on foreign trade and world markets have been provided by the KOPINT Market Research Institute. Forecasts published by the Research Institute of Finance have been based on a detailed analysis of recent crisis phenomena.

Since 1967, the Economic Research Institute (ERI) established at the Central Statistical Office, has made regular short term forecasts for the government two or three times a year. While the NPO's forecasts (in their final forms) reflected, first of all, the central wishes of politicians, the main task of ERI has been to reveal inconsistencies in the target growth path by taking into account micro-level information from the different sectors – households, enterprises, financial institutions, etc.

The traditional way of planning by the NPO was to build up input-output tables from sectorial expert's estimations and centrally-decided targets for domestic demand. Plan targets were also set for the main aggregates of the system of national accounts, such as sources and uses of GDP, budget incomes and receipts. In addition, the NPO has developed a number of other techniques, including linear programming, econometric, time series, ARIMA and dynamic factor models, for forecasting macroeconomic development. Hitherto, however, policymakers have been rather reluctant to pay attention to the predictions made by these different methods because, after all, the target values of the national plans have been decided by the political authorities.

The ERI forecasts have taken into account consultations with policymakers in government offices, but principally they have been based on business survey data and round table interviews with representatives of companies, banks, etc. The ERI forecasts have been presented in quarterly ERI reports showing the annual GDP forecast modified on the basis of the most recent quarterly information and describing the main tendencies of business cycle derived from the analysis of the behaviour of economic agents. Methodological development of the ERI forecasts has started with the elaboration of the ERI annual econometric macromodel.

III. Information base of forecasts made by ERI

ERI's forecasting methodology

The structure of the present information system used for forecasts made by ERI is shown in Chart 1, which also demonstrates the forecasting process.

Up to now, the ERI's forecasting methodology has been flexible. The Central Statistical Office publishes macro data according to the UN System of National

Chart 1. **Composition of ERI forecasts**

Macro-level information

FORECASTED GDP BALANCE
(for the current year)

Consultations with ministerial experts of:

- macro-economic planning
- budgetary finances
- international indebtedness
- foreign trade

Annual historical data concerning:

- the balance of Gross Domestic Product (GDP)
  private consumption
  government expenditures
  investments
  change in the inventory investments and net exports
    by rouble and non-rouble settlements

Annual forecasts of the ERI econometric model.

BUSINESS CYCLE

Monthly statistical data concerning:

- growth rates and prices of industrial production and construction
- state purchase of agricultural products;
- investments (excluding private investments) by decision making authorities
- foreign trade commercial orders by branches
- exports and imports by commodities and groups of countries
- retail trade turnover and prices
- households' money incomes
- internal and external indebtedness

Micro-level information

Interviews with firms' and banks' representatives

Data concerning finances, production factors and sales of firms

Business survey data covering:

- around 1 000 enterprises in industry, construction and retail trade (annual surveys)
- around 100-150 enterprises (twice a year)

Accounts (SNA). The time series used to track the business cycle (except for the components of GDP) have been changing, following changes in the economic system. Data concerning money balances, different types of loans, financial market variables, etc., are now relevant and have become available in the last year or two. Because there has not been a stable set of leading indicators, it has not been feasible to devise a composite index for forecasting the business cycle. All the above information are integrated by ERI's researchers in a traditional way, that is by analysing new data and emerging adjustment processes. In addition, the lack of a standard methodology has been due to the importance of political pressures on forecasting activity up to recent times. Several statistical problems have to be solved in order to assure the comparability and homogeneity of time series, which is a precondition for developing a standard methodology. The requirements for development of statistics will be analysed in the next part.

Development of the ERI's forecasting system should be concentrated around two of the existing elements. These are **business surveys** and **model building**. Business surveys have to be modified to take account both of new features of the Hungarian economy and of methodological requirements so that they can be used for comparative computation over longer periods. The ERI annual macromodel, built up around the balance of GDP, has to become the core of a short term forecasting system based on disaggregated monthly or quarterly time series.

Business surveys

Since 1968, the annual business surveys have been carried out among about 1 000 enterprises, including 600-700 industrial firms, at the beginning of the year. Following recent institutional changes, surveys have been extended to cover cooperatives and new ventures of different types. The ERI annual questionnaire consists of two main parts. Questions concerning actual and planned production, sales, investments, profitability and financial resources available can be found in the first part. The second part contains the "qualitative" questions about managers' assessments of the present situation. Here there are questions designed to reveal difficulties such as shortages in demand or supply of inputs, technical level of products and capacity utilisation problems and to see how firms are making their growth projections covering employment, innovation, inventory investments, etc. Expectations about financial resources, demand and price changes are also reported.

In the half-yearly ERI business surveys, which cover 100-150 firms, the overwhelming majority of questions relate to current management problems. Topics investigated recently have included the employment and production consequences of the halt in rouble trade in January 1990 and liquidity problems caused by "queuing" as a result of the recent rapid expansion of trade credit. Experts from the Hungarian Chamber of Commerce have participated in the selection of these special topics.

Macromodel forecasts

The model is organised around the balance of GDP. The estimated behavioural equations relate to aggregate supply and to the components of final demand. The income generation and redistribution process is described by identities, using exogenously given parameters.

In the 1980s, Hungarian economic development could have been characterised as modest growth rate of domestic supply for most of the decade and stagflation at the end of the period. Since domestic demand could not be constrained to the planned level there was probably a permanent excess demand. The tension was even growing due to the restrictions on imports from convertible currency areas up to 1988. For the description of the disequilibrium between demand and supply, business survey data concerning capacity utilisation and expected input shortages have been used in the ERI macromodel. The model's general characteristics are given in Chart 2.

The model's predictions extrapolating past tendencies serve as a basis for the ERI's forecasts. These latter, however, go beyond the model by incorporating expectations of different agents and by taking into account interdependencies and shocks that did not exist in the observation period of the model.

Chart 2. **Main characteristics of the ERI macromodel**

Field	Macro-economic model of the Hungarian economy.
Endogenous variables	– Aggregate supply – Components of domestic final demand (private consumption, investment) – Foreign trade (exports and imports) – Variables of the income generation and redistribution process.
Type	Econometric model.
Utilisation	Policy evaluation and forecast.
Data base	Annual data on national balances at current and 1981 prices.
Observation period	1970-1987
Forecast period	2-3 years
Disaggregations	– Economic agents (households, firms, government) – Investments by decision-making authorities (firms and the State) – Exports and imports settled in rouble and in non-rouble currencies.
Size	Around 25 equations of which 9 are econometrically estimated.
Estimation method	Ordinary least squares.
Exogenous variables	– Domestic and world market prices – Policy variables – Business survey data – Foreign indebtedness – World market demand.
Computer management system	Estimation, simulations and forecasts have been made by using TSP 4.1 version software.

IV. ERI's new tasks and statistical requirements

Increasing demand for short term forecasts can be expected in Hungary because of moves towards a market economy. Having lost its priority in directing the economy, the task of central planning is now to make indicative plans for the orientation of the economic actors. The relationship between national planning and forecasting has been reversed: the target values of national development should be derived from forecasts of different time horizons. In addition, not only the central authorities but different economic agents (banks, enterprises) are expected to be interested in forecasting.

Forecasts made by using different theoretical approaches and methods will be needed. As a consequence of changes, ERI forecasts will, in future, have to give great prominence to the description of the business cycle. For this purpose, using the actual information system of ERI, a computation system of forecasts for regular utilisation will have to be constructed.

Two parts can be distinguished within this computation system:

– *Set of leading indicators:*

  Three data sets: annual data available for 1960-1989;
  monthly data for 1979:1-1990:6
  business survey data annual – for 1968-1990 semi-annual – for 1989:1-1990:1;

  Composite indicators of business cycle

  Forecasting business cycle by leading indicators.

– *Model building for short term forecasting*
  - on the basis of monthly time series;
  - using panel data from company managers.

The structure of the forecasts made by the ERI are no longer connected to the short term plans. In addition, it must be noted that no quarterly or monthly data are available on GDP and its demand components according to the structure of the annual national accounts. For this reason, a system of monthly time series would fit better with business cycle analysis in the future. The GDP accounts can be considered as a framework for annual medium term forecasts, but it seems to be better to look for some other reference series or a set of series which is available monthly. Decision can be made about the reference series and chronology only after time series analysis of data. Unfortunately, we have only got annual business survey data for a long period and so the majority of the leading indicators will have to be obtained from the existing statistical monthly data. One of the main tasks for ERI is the development of six-monthly business surveys, which is creating some financial difficulties at this time.

Since, generally, monthly data are available only for the 1980s, annual data have to be used for the analysis of longer run economic cycles. It can be seen from the flow chart of the ERI forecasting (Chart 1) that the content of the available monthly data differs a lot from the annual national accounts data. Some of the basic ratios are given in the following table to illustrate the order of differences.

Further problems of statistical inference are caused by the lack of time series on some basic aspects of the emerging market processes. Data on loans, interest rates, money balances, tourist expenditures by Hungarian citizens and unemployment are

Table 1. **Ratios of monthly data (*) to annual aggregates (+)**
Per cent, in 1988

Industrial production(*)/total output(+)	47.8
Industrial value added(+)/GDP(+)	30.6
Retail trade turnover(*)/private consumption(+)	81.3
Investments of state-owned firms(*)/total(+) (including private investments as well)	78.3
Households' money incomes(*)/households' income(+)	84.0

examples. From a methodological point of view, these problems can be summarised as problem of indicator construction and of modelling with an incomplete data base, but behind this, there are at least three different questions to be answered.

The first problem is a **theoretical** one: how to make forecasts in a period of transition. How to take into account in forecasts data representing interdependencies that did not exist in a centrally-planned economy. These partly missing data are, for example, regulators of a financial character, notably short and long term interest rates and their effects on saving and investment. Often the nature of the relation can be supposed to have changed (e.g. taxation and subsidization). Changes in economic conditions make it necessary to analyse the reaction of different economic actors. Indicators of the economic behaviour of agents, such as different elasticities and propensities must be derived. For this reason, up to now, construction of composite indicators which both describe and forecast the business cycles has failed.

In the past, a lack of economic theory or ideological constraints have paralysed modelling. Now, the shortness of the period of observation of the new economic processes creates difficulties in developing new methods and models. Econometric models used for forecasts will obviously have to be revised to take account of structural changes. There are, however, some aspects of the Hungarian economy where econometric model building on the basis of monthly data can be successful. Modelling of private consumption on the basis of different models of consumer choice seems to be appropriate for short term forecasts. Again, instead of using time series of short or incomplete observations periods, panel data concerning management problems can be used for the estimation of behavioural equations for the business sector.

The second type of missing data problem is related to the **structural changes** of the Hungarian economy. Transformation of ownership should result in a reduction of state-owned enterprises and big cooperatives from their 90 per cent share of 1989. At present, there are no reliable statistics concerning the management of the expanding private sector. Adjustment to structural change is one of the main task of statistical development. The main tendencies in structural transformation are illustrated in Table 2.

Structural change should be taken into account in the ERI's business surveys as well. This means that our business surveys will have to cover all the different sectors of the economy – state-owned, privatised, joint ventures, and small enterprises.

Table 2. **Changes in the number of business entities**

	1986	1987	1988	1989	1990
Number of business entities (corporate bodies only)	7 916	8 578	9 597	10 811	15 235
Foundation	849	1 163	1 445	4 669	1 953
New	747	1 085	1 377	4 578	1 753
Liquidation	187	144	231	245	99
Without legal successor	94	72	87	166	36

Source: *Monthly Statistical Bulletin*, Central Statistical Office, Budapest, n°5, 1990.

The third group contains questions of **measurement**, which is underlined by the accelerating inflation in Hungary. For the analyses of chronology and interdependencies of economic processes, the volume and price effects have to be identified. The monthly statistical data available are generally valued at current price. Monthly time series of the corresponding prices (if there are any) are published as 12 months' growth rates. For construction of a set of leading indicators, consistent time series of volume and price changes will have to be compiled on a monthly basis.

In addition to the above problems of partly missing data, there are some "blank areas" of statistics. Because of financial difficulties, household surveys have recently had to be postponed. The micro-simulation system used by the Central Statistical Office is based on data for 1985. The accuracy of these computations is clearly debatable. From the point of view of the ERI forecasts, it is important to have reliable information about behavioural characteristics of different social groups.

Although business cycles should be analysed on the basis of short-term data, because of the several problems described above, annual data will have to serve as benchmarks. Today, annual data on national accounts are released to users with a significant lag (2-3 years). Because of structural changes the number of business entities has multiplied. Data collection can be based on representative samples, and methods of data processing should be adjusted to the characteristics of the data. Establishing new data processing systems takes a longer time.

In this paper, the present statistical system in Hungary was considered as given. Now that it is no longer subject to political influences, the statistical system is changing and this may open up new possibilities for short-term forecasting. The ERI's projects described in this paper can be realised without difficulty by using statistical data presently available. If the data base can be improved – through greater reliability of both primary and computed statistics and more rapid publication – the forecasts made by ERI could be refined.

Agricultural Statistics in the USSR

Peter Aven
International Institute for Applied Systems Analysis, Austria

It is planned to restructure Soviet agriculture by increasing managerial independence and putting much greater reliance on price mechanisms. Statistics presently available on agriculture in the Soviet Union are not well adapted to designing such reforms nor to monitoring their implementation. In common with Soviet statistics in general, there is a serious lack of monetary information, in particular on costs of agricultural inputs and on the value of agricultural output. There is little information on the "private supplementary holdings" which now provide a third of basic foods. Data are not readily available to analyse the social, demographic and environmental aspects of agricultural production.

I. Introduction

The restructuring of the management and the entire economic mechanism of the agroindustrial complex, which is now underway in the Soviet Union, should bring appreciable expansion of the enterprises' managerial independence and greater emphasis on economic incentives and levers. This, however, require in-depth restructuring of the system of agricultural statistics, which is still in line with the traditional "administrative" managerial methods.

Generally speaking, the design of a statistical system mirrors the idea of what is crucial for the functioning of the object it describes and what objectives are to be pursued in controlling the object. At the same time, the design of the system is determined by the choice of means, method, control instruments, and by the type of the control system. This paper shows that the set of indicators shaping Soviet agricultural statistics not only mirrors its orientation towards exclusively maximising output, but also corresponds to the use of traditional methods for attaining this result.

II. Paradoxes of soviet agricultural statistics

An analysis of Soviet agricultural statistics reveals several paradoxes. The list of them described below is certainly incomplete, but it shows how the set of indicators used has helped to create the problem facing Soviet agriculture.

Incomplete information and redundant data

The system of Soviet agricultural statistics is build up hierarchically. All information about the "higher echelons" (districts, regions and republics) is made up of data received from the farm level and is taken from annual reports from the collective and state farms. As they are transferred to subsequent stages, data are aggregated and a great part of them lost, while practically no new information is obtained. As a result the vast and clearly redundant amounts of data obtained from the farms (their annual reports include over 300 indicators), eventually prove insufficient for analysis and control at the level of the republics or the USSR as a whole.

An example of harmful data transformation is provided by statistics of cereal yields. Information on gross harvests, land sown for cereals (and thus on their yields) is requested from the farms. In the meantime, the Central Statistical Agency cites in its publication the information on the average yields of cereals in the Union republics (NK, 1986). As there are large variations around the average crop yields, this indicator is not very informative. It can then be concluded that such information should either not be requested from the farms, or the original, unaggregated information should be published.

Another example of "redundant" information is provided by the data, which is also requested from the farms, on the distribution of workers between agricultural sectors. These data are actually unavailable at the district level. As a consequence, on the one hand the opinion is that too many reports are requested from the farms, whilst, on the other hand the specialists in rural economics are short of crucial information.

"Extensive" indicators in conditions of intensification

Despite the move to intensification by the agrarian economy, the set of statistical indicators reflect the old-fashioned orientation of agricultural development being linked to boosting output regardless of inputs. The bulk of the statistical reports contain information on croplands, gross harvest, earnings from the sale of produce, etc. Considerably less attention is given on the costs component. In the farms' annual reports, less than 10 indicators show expenditures on material inputs. Moreover, expenditures on some resources (such as mineral fertiliser and plant protection chemicals) are not reflected in the statistical reports (the Central Statistical Agency only cites data on their supplies for agriculture). In this connection it is practically impossible to objectively determine the efficiency of agricultural production. This is greatly exacerbated by the problems of pricing and by the lack of estimates of resource potential. Also "extensiveness" is clearly seen in the domination of stock indicators over flow indicators. Thus, information on machinery inputs and discards, herd reproduction, and on the fodder balance, etc., is partially absent. This shows not only the common desire for fast results irrespective of the losses incurred, but also provokes uneconomical use of material resources.

Lack of monetary information

The current restructuring of the economic mechanism is intended to produce an expansion of the role which money plays in the development and control of production. However, Soviet agricultural statistics reflect the long-standing idea of the socialist economic mechanism as a "command-directed economy", in which money plays a formal, secondary role. Despite the greater emphasis on the profitability of agricultural enterprises, and despite the need to enhance the role of credit and prices, the present-day statistics contain no data on subsidies and credits, nor do they make it possible to estimate the role which these play in the production process of today. Actually, from the multitude of monetary indicators obtained, our statistics trace (and this only at the farm level) only the costs of various products and of payment for work. The latter naturally reflects the fact that "wage fund controls" remain, together with the directive setting of plans, as the main method of controlling the system.

Lack of information for interregional comparisons

Comparison of the production conditions, processes, and results between different regions is a key instrument of economic analysis. However, Soviet agricultural statistics do not provide an opportunity for such comparisons. It is planned to publish totals and averages for the union republics, which at he moment is obviously insufficient, and also on regions and even rural districts. Detailed information for small areas is essential for comparative analyses. Although the national level data are produced from the data provided by the regions, these latter are not published by the authorities.

The lack of objective information on the specifics and comparative efficiency of agricultural production in different regions is one reason why agricultural practices which have proved their worth in some regions are enforced on other regions where they are totally unsuitable. This is an explanation for the fixing of local norms, for so-called improvement of the national regulations, etc.

Supply and demand statistics

The existing system of agricultural statistics mirrors the trend towards expansion of output without sufficient attention being given to questions of efficiency. It is difficult to see from the published data how the agricultural system functions – how the products are distributed and how consumption differs between the regions, or between income, age and other social groups. In this connection it is difficult to forecast, for example, the effects of raising the prices of particular food products in line with wage rises, as proposed by some economists (see for example, Shatalin, 1986).

In addition, it cannot be understood from the existing statistics how this, or other economic policies, might affect the behaviour of collective and state farms. Above all, the distribution of products between the different channels of sale has not to date shown up in the statistical reports. (At the moment all the farms produce in excess of the plan and 30 per cent of the plan purchases of potatoes, vegetables, fruits and berries can be sold outside the system of state purchases.) It is, therefore, difficult to see how various products are distributed between the different sale channels.

Lack of data on Private Supplementary Holdings

Private Supplementary Holdings (PSH) are today an independent and essential sector of Soviet agricultural production, functioning quite separately from the public sector. "Without the PSH, per capita consumption of the basic foods would be one third below the present level. To keep food consumption at the existing level without the PSH help, the collective and state farms would have to nearly double the area sown to labour-intensive crops and to increase the population of productive livestock by 20 per cent and the aggregate labour inputs by approximately one-third" (see Kalugina, 1984). However, statistics have neglected the PSH. From the published data, it is impossible to understand how the PSHs are financed, how the workers' incomes are determined and how produce is distributed, or to compare the efficiency of the PSH and the public sector. Information on comparative efficiency acquires special importance in farming policies to shift agriculture from central planning to a system of economic competition by producers with the state's indicative influence.

Lack of social and ecological long-term sustainability indicators

A crucial problem of rural development is that of the long-term sustainability of agriculture. Since the beginning of the 19th century, agriculture in the majority of the industrialised countries has been an object of rapid intensification. The aggregate inputs of labour and capital have been rapidly rising per hectare and falling per unit of output. During the past 40-50 years this process has been developing especially rapidly. In the beginning, the growth of material expenditure in agriculture was accompanied by relative (and even absolute) migration of the workforce. Since 1950, the area sown for cereals has increased by only 22 per cent, but increases in consumption of energy in agriculture, use of tractors, and mineral fertiliser inputs have resulted in a threefold increase in the production of cereals (see Meadows, 1987).

However, such intensification has given rise to new problems of rural development. The first group of such problems is related to environmental pollution and degradation of the main resources of agricultural production – soil and water. Among the indicators of such degradation are soil erosion, secondary salinisation and growing acidity of soil, depletion of soil humus, growing aridity, depletion of fresh water resources, etc. The importance of this process can hardly be overestimated. In Poletayev (1985), references to data presented elsewhere by A.L. Yanshin and V.A. Kovda shows that over the last 30-40 years the Russian black soil plains have lost one-third of their humus and their fertile layer has thinned by 10-15 cm (natural rehabilitation of the fertile layer takes over 100 years). A loss of 1 mm of the upper fertile layer is equivalent to a yield loss of 10 kg/hectare of maize and 8 kg/hectare of wheat, soya, sorghum and oats. This means that due to humus losses alone the cereal yields in the black soil zone of the USSR are tens of kg per hectare less than potential yields.

The ecological and soil problems are not the only result of agricultural intensification. The other set of problems are of a social nature. Some of them are related to the impact of some new agricultural technologies on the health of the rural population. Thus the negative effects of cotton defoliants have of late been extensively discussed in the Soviet press. Other problems are brought about by the stratification of the rural population, agroindustrial integration, the breakdown of traditional village communities, rural exodus, etc. Of course, it is not production intensification in itself, but the choice of particular technologies, that determines the intensity of such processes. For example, center-pivot irrigation has accelerated the growth of unemployment and the easing out of the small-scale farms from the agricultural sector of the United States.

At present, agricultural statistics reflect the traditional orientation towards economic results without attempting to measure externalities of this kind. The statistics produced on the basis of farms' annual reports contain no social indicators nor information on soil and climate potential and quality of the environment. If such information is occasionally collected, it lives a life of its own and is independent from the economic statistics and from the process of economic decision-making. This is shown by the inadequate use and often formal filling of the rural areas social forms.

III. Restructuring of agricultural statistics and regional monitoring

Reshaping agricultural statistics is an extremely difficult task, that cannot be implemented in the short term. The author of this paper does not assume that his description of the future programme for restructuring the Soviet agricultural system is complete. Here he raises the question of developing such a programme and outlines several aspects that should be taken into account. Three main approaches can be singled out. The first one is compilation of a set of indicators selected on the basis of their content. It would involve describing in words the meaning of a large range of data that are typically used as indicators of rural development. To broaden the coverage of the indicators, soil scientists, economists, and sociologists could be asked for their ideas about the most important factors behind agricultural development and which parameters should be followed.

The second approach consists of finding the most important factors on the basis of various simulation models of the rural sector.

The third, and in my opinion the most promising approach, involves the use of various formal statistical methods for analysing large arrays of empirical data, including factor and determinant analysis, principal components methods, expert evaluations and multidimensional scaling. These methods make it possible to:

- Estimate the "informativeness" of individual characteristics;
- Single out the "interconnected" indicators and thus avoid unwanted duplication in the system of indicators;
- Build new composite indicators, each of which represents a group of primary indicators and describes a specific aspect of the phenomenon under study.

Use of the third method of data analysis is in a sense "orthogonal" to the first; the conclusions from statistical analysis are determined by the discovery of relationships among the data and often run counter to common sense. In reality, the use of statistical methods certainly must be accompanied by content analysis.

It should be emphasised that the use of formal statistical methods of data analysis, just like the creation of simulation models, requires related information. This is supplied, as a rule, in the form of a matrix, the columns of which correspond to the indicators and the rows to the objects they describe. In the development of a system of agricultural statistics, the indicators are the potentially possible characteristics of rural development and the objects are particular farms or regions. The objects could be rural regions in selected European countries, preferably with different levels of output and productivity, which are thus converted into "experimental proving grounds" for designing a system of agricultural statistics.

In each of the experimental proving grounds, complete information must be gathered and it will then be analysed in order to single out the most important interconnections between individual characteristics. This will enable a "rural monitoring" system to be developed which should include the following information from each region:

- A system of primary signs which characterise all the potentially important matters relating to development of the rural sector;
- Information-collecting services;
- Software services for rapid processing of this information with the help of formal methods and for issuing it in the form required for control.

Considering that representatives of regional statistical departments are found in every district of the USSR, organisation of the "rural-monitoring" system in one, or several regions does not appear very labour-consuming, particularly as a sufficient number of software packages are available for statistical analysis.

It may be noted that practical use of the "rural-monitoring" system by the divisions in the selected regions and the analysis of the information requested will help better to understand what is seen as important from the viewpoint of decision-makers and what information is actually used for decision-making in the rural sector.

IV. Conclusion

Reorganisation of agricultural statistics is an essential phase in the integration of the economic, ecological and social policies in the rural sector of the economy. Immediate connection between integration and long-term sustainability of agricultural production necessitates such reorganisation. Reshaping the economic mechanism of the Soviet agroindustrial complex makes this even more necessary.

References

KALUGINA, Z.I. (1984), "Development problems of private supplementary holdings in Siberian villages", *Izvestia of the Siberian Branch of the USSR Academy of Sciences*, Economics and Applied Sociology series, n° 1, Issue 1.

MEADOWS, D.H. (1987), *Sustainability of agriculture: the state of technology, the state of US practice, and possible options of IIASA*. Paper prepared for the IIASA Food and Agriculture Programme Meeting, Sopron.

NK (1986) *Narodnoe Khoziaistov SSSR v 1985*, (translation: Soviet economy in 1985), Financy i Statistika, Moscow.

POLETAYEV, P. (1985), *Ratsionalnoe Prirodopolzovanie v Ostraslakh APK*, (translation: Rational use of nature in agroindustrial complex sectors), Ekonomika Selskogo Khozaistva, 18.

SHATALIN, S.S. (1986), *Sotsialnoe Razvitie i Ekonomicheski Rost* (translation: Social development and economic growth), Communist, 14.

Macro-Economic Statistics Required by the International Monetary Fund: Transition Issues in Central and Eastern European Countries

International Monetary Fund, Washington D.C.

In accordance with the obligations of the IMF's Articles of Agreement, member countries provide to the Fund a wide range of economic statistics, including those relating to money and banking, government finance, the balance of payments, national accounts and other real sector statistics. In the first three areas the Fund has developed methodologies and guidelines that permit data to be presented in an internationally comparable form. As regards money and banking statistics, a major problem for the CEECs is that the meaning of the data will change as the structure of their unitary banking systems is transformed to a market basis. Government finance statistics in the CEECs are often difficult to interpret because present accounting rules allow transaction records to be transferred between accounting periods and because of the absence of a standardised basis for recording transactions. Balance of payment statistics suffer, inter alia, from the existence of multiple exchange rates. The paper argues that for the purposes of policy making and analysis, highest priority should be given to the adoption of internationally recognised methodologies including the SNA and the IMF's related statistical systems.

I. Introduction

It is appropriate that at an early stage in the process of moving from central planning to a market system, the countries of Central and Eastern Europe should place a high priority on identifying statistical needs and on developing and implementing a programme that establishes the framework and the enabling mechanism to meet them. Policymakers as well as other users of statistics in these countries will undoubtedly experience difficulties arising from the absence or inadequacy of data as these economies move to market systems. At the broadest level, the policy dialogue now taking place as part of the reform process underscores the importance of establishing a coherent and consistent set of macro-economic statistics. It is also important to recognise the special circumstances that exist throughout the period of transition, in which statistics compiled in accordance with a central planning regime will continue to be produced, although in modified form, alongside newly developed statistics resulting from the move to a market system. To facilitate the integration of the Central and Eastern European countries into the world economy, the development of new statistical systems should be based upon internationally agreed statistical methodologies, and it is in this area that the international statistical agencies can provide support. Several of these countries have already taken some first steps in moving from the Material Product System (MPS) to the System of National Accounts (SNA). This paper deals with the issues that will arise in this changing environment, focusing particular attention on the related statistical systems in the areas of balance of payments, money and banking, and government finance developed by the Fund.

II. Statistical requirements of IMF

The Articles of Agreement of the fund define the institution's role in gathering and disseminating statistics relating to its member countries. Article VIII, Section 5(a) (reproduced in Annex 1) sets forth the obligations incurred by members in furnishing the Fund with information needed for its activities and encompassing the provision of national data on a wide range of topics. Article VIII furthermore prescribes that the Fund shall act as a centre for the collection and exchange of information on monetary and financial matters. Data reported to the Fund are required in fulfilment of its responsibilities to oversee the international monetary system in order to ensure its effective operation, to conduct surveillance over members' exchange rate and other policies, and in order to conduct its financial operations with members. On joining the Fund, a member country enters into arrangement to report to the Fund regularly on a wide range of economic and financial statistics. The statistical needs of the Fund cover the regular reviews of individual member country economies (Article IV consultations), analyses in connection with countries' requests for financial assistance through the use of the Fund's resources, global analyses that are embodied in the World Economic Outlook, policy and systemic studies related to the international financial system, and the maintenance of the comprehensive country and world databases of internationally comparable statistics that are presented in the Fund's statistical publications.

The Fund has developed statistical systems and the underlying methodologies in the fields of balance of payments, monetary and fiscal statistics. In the review of the SNA now in progress, considerable effort is being made to harmonise the new version of the SNA with the Fund's statistical methodologies which are themselves in varying stages of review and revisions. These are *The Balance of Payment Manual*, 4th Edition, 1977; *A Manual on Government Finance Statistics,* 1986; and *A Draft Guide to Money and Banking Statistics in International Financial Statistics*, 1984.

For several of the countries of Central and Eastern Europe that have been members of the Fund for some years, statistical reporting and data exchange arrangements with the Fund have been in effect from an early stage of membership. Effective membership dates for these countries are as follows: Hungary (6 May 1982), Poland (12 June 1986); Romania (15 December 1972); and Yugoslavia (27 December 1945). Data reporting in the period prior to the recent intensification of the move to a market system has been in terms of the existing centrally-planned economic structure, adapted when necessary to bring the macro-economic aggregates to a state that permits analysis and comparison in an intercountry and global context. For these countries, and for Bulgaria and the Czech and Slovak Federal Republic, which have recently applied to join the Fund, there is the twofold task in the period ahead of recasting the statistical processes to meet the needs of the market system and, in the indeterminate period of the transition, to devise ways of assembling data collected under the old and new systems to meet the needs of policy and analysis.

III. Financial statistics

The transformation of the financial systems of the Central and Eastern Europe countries will require significant changes in the system of financial statistics. Replacement of the unitary banking system and the centralised system of credit allocation by a financial system that encompasses an array of financial intermediaries and indirect monetary instruments will bring with it demands for new forms of statistical information. The specific features of the new system will differ from country to country and will depend on a number of political and legal decisions. Nonetheless, a major difficulty in all of these countries will be the existence, for a time, of continued financial relationships between economic agents which have been carried over from the planning system and which have not or cannot be converted readily in accordance with a market system.

It can be expected that with the transition process will come regulations and appropriately devised guidelines for supervision, governing prudential aspects of risk assessment, and capital adequacy. This will require new forms of statistical reporting aimed at providing analytically useful data on financial claims, covering also their maturity, liquidity, and frequency of turnover.

During the transition, banks are likely to be faced with a two-tier system of transactions. For statistical purposes, stocks and flows (transactions) that continue to relate to the central planning process will need to be reported on the basis of administrative records. In some cases, the owner of a financial asset, and the ultimate obligor, may not be identifiable. Thus, the balance sheets of financial institutions will constitute an admixture of the old and the new, for which statistical reporting increasingly will need to reflect the development of balance sheet positions that derive from market-based financial decisions. As a prior requirement, for bank supervision as well as for policy formulation and analysis, the establishment of new forms of statistical reporting will be dependent upon the creation of a new basic accounting plan that will permit identification of the key monetary items of account and the development of a consolidated set of broad monetary aggregates. In structuring the new accounting plan, provision should be made for the identification of accounts carried over from the pretransition period.

The process of transition will yield data that will be difficult to compare. In a period-to-period comparison the meaning of the principal aggregates will change as financial claims accumulated under the planning process are replaced by those created as a result of the market mechanism. The aggregates themselves will reflect the changing institutional structures and the changing mix of financial instruments. For this reason, it may be desirable to continue for a time with separate reporting by banks to identify separately transactions and accounts that continue to reflect the central planning system and those stemming from the move to a market system.

The desirability of separate reporting during the transition can be related to a number of balance sheet items, the nature of which would change dramatically with reform. Banks' deposits with the State Bank under central planning, representing surplus funds in the economy, will need to be distinguished from banks' minimum reserves required on market-related bank deposit liabilities after the reform of the financial system.

Difficulties will also exist in obtaining a comprehensive coverage of claims on, and liabilities to, government. A particular problem surrounds the separation of the production activities of government (the enterprise sector) and the functions of the government. Privatisation and denationalisation of state enterprises will bring added complications in this area.

Yet another problem can be identified in the form of loan balances for the production sector under central planning that are non-performing or in arrears. Until these loans have been written off, rescheduled, or otherwise dealt with, they should be reported separately from the stock of claims arising from market-based lending by banks.

Clearing balances accumulated in the accounts of banks will also require a continuation of separate reporting. These balances are likely to persist in balance sheets, since the process of reform will make it difficult to establish who is obligated to make final settlement.

IV. Fiscal statistics

Under central planning, fiscal activities and fiscal policy were directed to the implementation of the plan. Given the wide-ranging nature of government activities in these countries, government operations required comprehensive and detailed reporting which was geared largely to meeting administrative needs. The resulting data systems did not attempt to produce the types of data needed to develop, implement, and monitor fiscal policy. However, as the Fund has already determined in its operational work with a number of these countries, this detailed information, if appropriately exploited, can be reorganised in accordance with the Fund's Government Finance Statistics (GFS) system in a manner that would facilitate its use for policy and analysis. At the same time, as noted below, attention will need to be given to deficiencies in the available statistics in these countries that relate to coverage, timing, and the basis of reporting.

Coverage problems result from the fact that only a portion of the government sector, as defined in the GFS system, is treated as such and is covered by the budgetary reporting system. For the operations of those governmental units and organisations not covered by the budget, there are problems with the availability of data and its quality, and the consistency of accounting standards. Year-to-year variations in the entities covered by the state budget raise difficult problems of consistency in the coverage of the government sector which will need to be addressed in the transition period.

Problems have also been observed in the compilation of data in the centrally-planned economies because of the lack of timely reporting. In addition, these countries have often followed the practice of applying an extended complementary period after the end of the fiscal year to record transactions related to that fiscal year, and at times of also using a reverse complementary period by which expenditures in one fiscal year were assigned to the following year. Such accounting devices are not consistent with the needs of fiscal analysis. This could also be said of the practice of applying varying reporting bases for government transactions, in which some accounts are reported on a cash basis, some on an accrual basis, and others on an appropriation basis.

Finally, the lack of information on government operations on a sub-annual basis will be a problem given the difficulties of making complex coverage adjustment on a quarterly or monthly basis. This, of course, is also a problem in countries other than those operating under central planning.

V. Balance of payments accounts

For the countries of Central and Eastern Europe that are members or prospective members of the Fund, balance of payment accounts are compiled mainly using the foreign exchange record system, although some use is made of other official data sources. On occasion, international trade statistics constitute the source of the merchandise account while at times other sources, including information from specialised financial institutions, are used. Other data sources that form the basis of balance of payments statistics in other economies, both developed and developing (transaction records, official administrative records, business surveys), do not generally form part of the information base in centrally-planned economies. In some countries balance of payments statistics are produced on a cash and on an accrual basis, the latter on an annual basis. As a rule, balance of payments accounts in these countries have been compiled for transactions in convertible currencies and for those in non-convertible currencies.

In the transition period the Fund will be working with these countries to comprehend better the balance of payments methodology now in use, and to identify new data sources that may be needed. As the move to a market system proceeds, and with the elimination of exchange controls, new data sources to replace the exchange records will be needed, a situation that has been faced by many other countries, including countries elsewhere in Europe. The balance of payments accounts themselves will become more complex as economic agents enter into a greater variety of transactions in both the current and capital account. In addition, for countries operating with a currency that is not fully convertible, there will remain the problem during transition of determining an appropriate exchange rate for use in the compilation of the balance of payments. In some cases, this problem is addressed through the application of a unitary (commercial) rate and through the compilation of the accounts in a major currency (e.g., in US dollars). It should be noted, however, that compilation problems arising from the existence of multiple exchange rates remains an important issue for many countries as the Fund proceeds with the revision of the *Balance of Payments Manual* and the *Guide to the Compilation of the Balance of Payments.*

VI. The tasks during transition

Some difficult choices will be facing the authorities in the transition period. Three sets of needs can be identified: (1) analysing historical statistics to refine their classification in order to derive as much historical continuity as possible; (2) developing a new system of methodologies and reporting systems for the period in which the economy has become predominantly market-based; and (3) producing temporary reporting systems for the transitional period, based on at times inappropriately constructed or partial information. Given the speed with which some governments are moving to implement the market system, priority should be given to developing new reporting systems and applying internationally agreed methodologies to compile analytically useful aggregates. The adoption of the SNA and the Fund's related statistical systems, and the production of internationally comparable statistics, will also have the benefit of facilitating the integration of these economies with the rest of the world. In all cases new statistical systems will require a good legislative base, appropriate protection of confidential data, well-designed and tested collection/reporting forms, processing and data dissemination systems, and the application of proven technology for processing.

On a final note, statistical systems, whether those of planned or market-based economies, should never be seen as static. As statistical methodologies periodically need revision to reflect development and change, so too do the related statistical systems. This may be some comfort to those countries now in the process of rapid change.

Annex 1

International Monetary Fund

Articles of Agreement

Article VIII: General obligations of members.
Section 5 : Furnishing of information.

a) **The Fund may require members to furnish it with such information as it deems necessary for its activities, including, as the minimum necessary for the effective discharge of the Fund's duties, national data on the following matters:**

i) Official holdings at home and abroad of (1) gold, (2) foreign exchange;

ii) Holdings at home and abroad by banking and financial agencies, other than official agencies, of (1) gold, (2) foreign exchange;

iii) Production of gold;

iv) Gold exports and imports according to countries of destination and origin;

v) Total exports and imports of merchandise, in terms of local currency values, according to countries of destination and origin;

vi) International balance of payments, including (1) trade in goods and services, (2) gold transactions, (3) known capital transactions, and (4) other items;

vii) International investment position, i.e., investments within the territories of the member owned abroad and investments abroad owned by persons in its territories so far as it is possible to furnish this information;

viii) National income;

ix) Price indices, i.e., indices of commodity prices in wholesale and retail markets and of export and import prices;

x) Buying and selling rates for foreign currencies;

xi) Exchange controls, i.e., a comprehensive statement of exchange controls in effect at the time of assuming membership in the Fund and details of subsequent changes as they occur; and

xii) Where official clearing arrangements exist, details of amounts awaiting clearance in respect of commercial and financial transactions, and of the length of time during which such arrears have been outstanding.

III

Strategies for Developing New and Better Statistics

Soviet Statistics: Needs, Plans and Progress

State Committee of the USSR on Statistics, Moscow

The paper lists the demands for new kinds of economic, financial and social statistics resulting from moves to a regulated market economy. It describes the steps that have already been taken to meet these new needs – notably in the areas of national accounts and price statistics – and lists the numerous problems that remain to be solved.

I. Changes in the need for data

The various measures for the transition to a regulated market economy now under way in this country have brought about radical changes in the work programme of the State Committee of the USSR on Statistics (Goskomstat). There has been a dramatic increase in interest, on the part of government bodies and the public, in macro-economic indicators, price indices and financial and social statistics. This has been accompanied by a certain weakening of interest in industrial/technical information.

The basic new requirements for statistics are the following:

a) Studies in the field of new property relations; reducing the role and scope of state property; developing new forms of management and business activity; acquiring basic indicators characterising such forms of property as state, cooperative, individual, etc. Data on state enterprises, the activities of which are regulated by unions, Republics, and local administrative bodies, also need to be revised.

b) Analysis of competition processes under conditions of economic independence, monopolistic production and the effectiveness of anti-monopolistic laws. Comparative analyses of effectiveness of enterprises belonging to different forms of property and management.

c) Further statistical studies of the consumer market and the market for factors of production; working out balances, at constant prices, of production and distribution; analysis of money capital of enterprises in comparison with the opportunities in the market for investment goods. Collecting data on the development of all forms of trade.

d) Studying financial aspects of production, including the state financial balance, the financial balances of the Republics and the financial balances of regions; analysis of the state budget deficit and its processes; money in circulation and the rates of its circulation; analysis of the establishment and functioning of the securities market, credit and tax policy. Organising data collection from banks and financial bodies.

e) A separate problem is constituted by such issues as monetary income of households, distribution of long-term loans, government fixed interest liabilities, shares of enterprises. In addition, the question of collecting information through tax declarations (of individuals) remains to be resolved.

f) A problem of cardinal importance is the problem of new price statistics, including the system of price indices based on representative items and deflator indices for macro-level estimates. It is necessary to organise the calculation of these indices since they are essential for the estimation of inflation rates and, consequently, for assessing the actual dynamics of economic processes.

g) The list of questions concerning studies of living standards of the population includes such items as compiling retail price indices for different socio-demographic groups of population; studying population groups with different levels of income, including the lowest one – pensioners. This has caused another problem – that of reorganising family budget statistics. A separate problem to resolve is the analysis of the effectiveness of measures for supporting low-paid households through provision of social guarantees.

h) It is considered necessary to organise studies of such issues as employment, unemployment, re-qualification and re-orientation of professional activities of the population, issues of labour force emigration and its internal migration.

i) Organising studies of the quality of the housing stock, expenditures on housing and also the question of satisfying housing needs.

j) In order to examine economic interrelations of the union Republics and interregional business links, it is considered necessary to organise data collection and processing for the analysis of regional exports and imports.

k) Organising data collection on the following questions: the national balance of payments; credit, debt and debt service; measuring purchasing power parities to provide a reliable comparison of macro-economic indicators with leading economically-developed countries.

At the present time there is a dramatic increase in interest by non-government organisations (primarily businesses and consumers) in statistical information that allows the new organisations to carry out their activities under a regulated market economy. In particular, there is a strong need for data on the activities of enterprises. There is also an insistent demand that, in solving all these problems, Goskomstat should make the transition to internationally approved principles and should adopt the statistical norms and standards of the United Nations and other international bodies drawing on the statistical experience of the countries with well-developed market economies.

II. The current state of Soviet statistics

A number of measures have been taken by Goskomstat in order to modify the structure and methodology of statistical information.

Work has begun on introducing the System of National Accounts (SNA) alongside the current system of the balance of the national economy (MPS), which is being preserved during the transition period. At the present time, Goskomstat – using SNA/MPS conversion keys – has begun to publish data on the Gross National Product. Estimates have been made of GNP by industry of origin and according to the structure of final expenditures.

A major new problem for Soviet statistics is the calculation of price indices based on the prices of representative items. During 1989, Goskomstat made estimates of the following indices:

- Retail price index for consumer goods and services purchased by households;
- Producer's price index for industrial production;
- Price index for agricultural production;
- Price index for transport services.

Methods have also been developed to compile price indices for deflating macro-economic aggregates.

Starting from 1990 foreign trade statistics have started to be compiled from customs declarations. Beginning in January 1991, the United Nations "Harmonised System" will be used for classifying imports and exports.

III. Strategy and problems in further developing Soviet statistics

The most rational approach to using the SNA, while preserving the MPS system, has been defined as the approach of "integrating the national economy". This is a deeper and a more sophisticated system of national economic accounting and involves developing an integrated system of macro-economic indicators. It provides for the coordination and interrelation of the concepts, definitions and classifications of the two systems in a single, unified and internally consistent system. On the macro level, such a system can be represented in the form of balance tables and accounts, inter-related by mutually coordinated concepts, definitions and classifications. This system will provide an extended and consistent picture of the economic process, with the sphere of material production being separately distinguished.

For the years 1990-1991, it is planned to develop a scheme of consolidated accounts at the macro-economic level – Gross Domestic Product, National Disposable Income, capital expenditures, and the balance of trade in goods and services. It is also planned to develop, during the same period, a scheme of accounts for separate sectors of the economy – accounts for production, accounts for expenditures on consumption and capital formation by industries and sectors, and accounts for the finance of capital expenditures by sectors.

In introducing the SNA and in integrating the SNA and MPS, an important place is devoted to input-output tables. Input-output tables coordinated with the SNA are to be compiled for the year 1992. To do this, it will be necessary to develop input-output tables according to the SNA, draw up lists of sectors (including sectors of the non-material sphere) and devise methods of providing the information base needed for the compilation of the SNA input-output tables.

Systematic development of the SNA requires a certain amount of work to be done in organising the SNA information base. In this connection it is necessary to reorganise and modify the system of accounting and statistical reporting towards international standards.

Taking into account the complex nature of the problems being faced by Goskomstat, we consider it would be very useful to organise groups of experts including both Soviet and Western experts, who would provide help and advice on a regular basis.

As problems of primary importance where we feel particular need for help, we would single out the following:

a) General problems of statistics:
   - *i)* Organising data collection for current statistics.
   - *ii)* Methodology and organisation of economic censuses.

b) Macro-economic (SNA) statistics:
   - *i)* Studying actual methods and data sources used in developing the SNA:
     - Applied to grouping data by sectors and industries in the accounts of production, consumption and capital formation, incomes and outlays and capital finance;
     - Applied to distinguishing between domestic and national economy.

c) Solving the questions of acquiring data on financial transactions from private companies.

d) Calculation of SNA indicators at the regional level (what indicators are to be developed at the level of union Republics, regions, and autonomous Republics?).

e) Problems connected with construction of indices for deflating macrolevel indicators including capital formation and for revaluing material stocks and fixed assets.

f) Price statistics:
   - *i)* Learning practical aspects of organising the collection of price statistics.
   - *ii)* Problems of precisely defining groups of representative goods and services; problems of widening the range of market services; problems connected with establishing the representative character of the goods and services included in the index; problems of selecting the enterprises for which prices are to be recorded.
   - *iii)* The problem of taking account of quality differences in estimating price indices.

g) Social statistics:
   - *i)* Learning the practical aspects of organising family budget surveys.
   - *ii)* Learning how to make sub-samples of family budgets for compiling a cost of living index.

h) Agricultural statistics:
   - *i)* The system of statistical observations of the activities of farms (sample or exhaustive); methods of farm selection in sample surveys; methods of estimating basic indicators of physical volumes of output and the system of estimating gross and final agricultural product.
   - *ii)* The practice of conducting agricultural censuses.

i) Labour statistics:

  i) The system of labour statistics indicators, such as indicators of employment, unemployment, professional qualifications and retraining of the labour force; intersectoral and interregional migration of labour force; wage and salary statistics.

j) Capital construction statistics:

  i) The system of data collection for capital formation by enterprises; statistics on fulfilment of state programmes in the field of capital construction; investment policy analysis.

k) Industrial statistics:

  i) Construction of volume indices of industrial production.

l) Trade statistics:

  i) Organisation of collection and processing of data on various trade and service statistics (sales, marketable resources, market services) under the regulated market economy.

  ii) Organisation of price observations for goods and services that form the basis for calculating price indices.

In our opinion, cooperation with Western experts should include the following elements: symposia, seminars, consultations, and exchange of experience on current and new statistical projects now being undertaken in the USSR.

Polish Statistics: Needs, Plans and Progress

Joseph Zajchowski
Central Statistical Office, Warsaw

The change from a supply-oriented to a demand-oriented economic system will involve a reduction, though not elimination, of physical production measures and considerably more emphasis on financial and economic statistics expressed in value terms. Unemployment and household budgets are identified as areas where more statistical enquiries are required. Financial statistics were almost completely ignored in the past but with the move to privatisation it is now urgent to collect information on the financial situation of enterprises.

The dramatic changes in the political and economic system which are taking place at present in Poland obviously have an impact on the objectives of statistics. The unprecedented character of these changes makes it difficult to use the experience of other countries and to grasp the full scope and details of the necessary adjustments to the statistical system. The experiences of the market economy countries may be useful in finding a solution to this problem but it seems that they cannot be transferred automatically without a second thought. First of all, due to the fact that our political and economic system is in a transition phase and secondly because the final shape of the new system has not yet been fully specified. It is reasonable to assume that for various reasons the new system will not be identical with the market economy systems existing in other countries. Besides, those systems differ from each other. That is why our ideas on the changes needed in Polish statistics should be viewed in the context of our theoretical analyses and observations and as a result of exchange of experience with selected market economy countries, such as West Germany, France, Austria and USA as well as with the Eurostat experts. Our approach will certainly change in the course of gaining our own practice and experience as well as working out a theoretical basis for our activities in this field.

Generally speaking, the adaptation of Polish statistics to the new political and economic system will be determined by two groups of factors: *i)* the necessity to cover new i.e. previously non-existent or marginal phenomena, and *ii)* the necessity to adjust the statistics to the new needs of both state administration and other actors in the socio-political system. Taking into account the present state of affairs in Polish statistics, it can be said that major changes determined by the above-mentioned factors should be introduced mainly in the area of economic rather than social statistics. We consider that surveys in the field of social statistics – demographic data, living conditions, prices and costs of living (even in conditions of high inflation), social services, health, education, culture, tourism and recreation conform with international standards. This is true both for the scope of the surveys, which cover practically all aspects of living conditions of the population, as well as the methods and organisation of surveys. It is obvious that there will also be changes in this area of statistics but it can be assumed that they will be of a quantitative rather than qualitative character.

Having made this general statement on the assumed evolution of social statistics we are aware of the necessity to introduce certain alterations and modifications also in this field. This concerns, first of all, the necessity to extend surveys on unemployment. Until now, this phenomenon did not exist in our country. It is possible to discuss hidden unemployment in the form of excessive employment both in industrial enterprises and in some agencies but the phenomenon was different in character from open unemployment. Besides, in Poland there were no statistical surveys to evaluate the scale and trend of excessive employment. As is well known, unemployment has occurred in Poland only in 1990 and at present it is still a rather small-scale phenomenon covering 2-3 per cent of the labour force outside agriculture. However, at present we are at the initial stage of working out a method for collecting information on the scale of this phenomenon. The information is collected from local administrative bodies which keep records of the number of unemployed. These bodies are at a stage of evolution which makes it difficult to set up a reliable data collection and processing system.

The next relevant, but poorly recognised problem, in the field of social statistics concerns incomes and expenditures of households, including households that own private enterprises. Until now, the budgets of this group of the population were not covered by surveys because it was a relatively small and irrelevant group from the economic point of view. However, it is expected that changes in the economic system will cause a rapid development of the private sector and an increase in the role of this group in the economy both with respect to the level and composition of demand as well as to the pattern and standard of consumption. Because of this, it is necessary to cover this group of households with statistical surveys. It is worth noting that, at present, statistical surveys cover neither the living conditions of this group nor economic transactions contracted between private units. Statistics cover only transactions concluded between the private and socialised sectors.

A problem which is on the border-line between social and economic statistics concerns the inclusion of the service sector into the system of national accounts. In Polish statistics the Material Product System (MPS) was applied for many years. According to this system, the units operating in the services sector were treated as using the outputs of the productive sphere i.e. they only took part in the process of distribution. When we adopt the SNA principles we will have to collect information on the units operating in the services sector in order to capture data needed for the national accounts. It can be added that the modifications are necessary not only because of the transition to the new system but also due to the increased commercialisation of social services.

As far as economic statistics is concerned the scale of indispensable changes seems to be much greater. The main cause of these changes is that users of statistics will need a different set of information as Poland moves from a supply-oriented to a demand-oriented system i.e. from a centrally-planned economy to a market type economy.

From the point of view of a statistical system, the supply-oriented economy required a different approach to the collection, processing and dissemination of information. It concentrated mainly on physical aspects of the production process – the material conditions and outputs. The financial and monetary aspects of economic phenomena and processes were of less importance – an exception to this rule being the surveys of household incomes and expenditures. However, these latter were incomplete because, as already mentioned, they did not cover transactions between units in the private sector. That is why it will be necessary to supplement and modify the present system of statistical information in order to be able to estimate adequately the level and composition of gross demand, the influence of governmental policy and the decisions of particular industrial enterprises. A special problem here is obtaining information on the financial situation of enterprises and its impact on the process of restructuring, bankruptcy, etc. It is possible that in future these problems will be of less importance but it seems that in the coming years and in the period of drastic changes in economic policy they will be very important. They are particularly vital for the administrative bodies responsible for financial policy in Poland i.e. the Central Bank and other financial institutions.

Financial statistics, especially for industrial enterprises, will have to be changed as far as the methodology and organisation of statistical surveys are concerned. The reform of the accounting and tax systems (adoption of VAT) which is under preparation is an additional complication. The implementation of these systems will bring our accounting and tax systems closer to the international standards. However, for the statistical services this means a necessity to work out a totally new reporting and data processing system.

The shift in the orientation of statistics towards the observation of demand and the factors determining it certainly does not mean that the observation of supply – or in broader terms of the material processes – will be abandoned. The problem is rather to find an answer to the question on how work in this area can be reduced, while still collecting information indispensable for an adequate evaluation of problems such as insufficient supply of means of production, bottlenecks or inadequate production of fixed assets.

Changes in ownership status will also create a demand for statistical information on both the scope as well as the economic and social consequences of privatisation. We have to start completely new surveys of the capital and monetary market and of interest rates. All of them need a corresponding methodological and organisational basis.

A characteristic feature of a statistical system oriented towards the supply and central distribution of goods was an emphasis on the collection and dissemination of data on the particular unit under observation rather than on its actual activities. The central management or – in broader terms – the state administration, was interested in the performance of each enterprise. The transition to the market economy system, and the decreased interference of the State in the economy, will shift the focus of statistics. This means that there will be a need to change the system of statistical classifications. The present system called the "Classification of the National Economy" is unit-oriented. In numerous cases a sector or branch covered units identified by their names – mainly industrial enterprises or their associations. Now we drop this classification and work on the adoption of the classification according to kind of activity. We plan to adopt the NACE system with slight modifications to take account of some specific features of the Polish economy.

The method of collecting data on small- and medium-sized enterprises, especially private ones, will also have to be changed. Outside agriculture, the share of the latter was negligible in our economy. The volume and structure of their economic activity were estimated mainly on the basis of the number of registered units and on relatively unreliable information on employment and the volume of sales to the socialised sector. The bias of the estimates was not relevant for the assessment of the level and composition of the social product generated and distributed. Due to the fact that the private sector is and will be developing in all branches of the national economy it is necessary to change the methods of statistical observation. We aim at covering the private sector with sample surveys and we plan to collect information on small-size units in the socialised sector in a similar way.

The basic problems which emerge in this connection are the following: achieving a necessary level of data reliability, the proper selection of representative units and an adequate frequency of surveys. The problems concerning the frequency of surveys is worth considering. In the centrally-planned economy there was a tendency towards a maximum frequency of data collection. This was justified by the need to provide the central authorities with data to let them react quickly to the current situation. An indirect consequence of this tendency was an attempt to cover all socialised units regardless of their size. It is expected that in the market economy the central administration will be less interested in very short-term information. On the other hand it seems that the enterprises forced to react to both long-term and short-term changes in the market will be more interested in such an information. It is obvious that the state statistics should not and does not have to satisfy all these needs but it cannot refrain from any reaction at all. Thus we have to face the problem of an adequate frequency of data collection and dissemination of information on particular economic phenomena. A wrong decision which prevents us from satisfying the genuine needs of users may, in our experience, force users to launch their own (even illegal) reporting systems.

In the context of the demand for statistical information, we are considering how far the statistical office should be involved in making economic projections. Until now only demographic projections were made. In other fields of statistics, no projections were attempted, other than some experimental work on research and development. It seems that in the market economy there are both the conditions and demand for short- and medium-term economic projections. An argument against undertaking them is the fact that the CSO projections are of an official and governmental character. This could place the office in a rather awkward position. The difficulty lies also in the lack of established procedures and the fact that, in the present state of the economy, the projections may not be very reliable. However, to meet the new demand we have already worked out a system of projections for industry.

Another problem which has to be solved in a different way than in the past concerns access to information on individual units of statistical observation. In the case of social and demographic surveys, this problem has been solved for good – information on individual units of observation is not released under any conditions. As far as enterprises are concerned, however, the situation is not so clear, especially in case of the state enterprises. In the past this problem was not fully recognised and there were ambiguities in this respect. On the one hand, excessive restrictions were imposed on information even at an aggregative level and this was justified by the alleged necessity to protect state secrets. On the other hand, a wide circle of users from the central administration as well as from political and social organisations had access to information on individual units. This caused ambiguity and uncertainty about the rules of access and dissemination of the results of statistical surveys.

The present tendency is to lift many restrictions on access to aggregated data. However, the problem of access to primary information is still unsolved. It is obvious that commercial and production secrets of particular units should not be disclosed, but the definitions here are not precise. Some information, especially on state enterprises, should be made available to the general public because of the need for public control of their activities. Due to the fact that what is and what is not a commercial or industrial secret is rather vague, it is hard to work out any precise definitions. We are aware of the opinion that no information on individual units collected by the statistical reporting system should ever be disclosed, but it seems that some exceptions should be allowed. Our doubts pertain mainly to the state enterprises, especially due to the fact that the public is deeply interested in the process of changing the ownership status and this interest can be satisfied only by providing information on particular units. It can be expected that the problem will become less important in the course of time and it will be possible to work on more rigorous rules for keeping secrets in economic statistics.

Romanian Statistics: Needs, Plans and Progress

National Commission for Statistics, Bucharest

The transition from a centralised to a democratic market system involves radical transformation of the statistical service in Romania, covering the legal framework, the sources and methods of data collection as well as the types of statistics collected. The paper describes the plans and progress to date in these various areas. Two urgent priorities are the calculation of price indices and coping with low response rates in enterprise surveys.

The historical and irreversible course to democracy in Romania, as a consequence of the People's Revolution at the end of December 1989, implies the transition from a hide-bound and hyper-centralised socio-economic system to a market economy. This necessarily entails reconsidering the structure of the statistical system.

The entire statistical information system will have to undergo a radical transformation. This requires a new legal framework which will determine the place and role of statistics within the state, which will ensure its autonomy and which will enhance its efficiency. Within its structure, our statistical system is to be adjusted to the new requirements at all stages, from data collection up to their dissemination and practical utilisation.

We are aware of the various problems which such a wide reform programme implies. They concern the real and specific conditions in our country and the available human, material and financial resources. We will need to determine the priorities in implementing the new system on the basis of a short- and long-term strategy and to define our options in finding solutions, taking into account the experience of the market economy countries.

We have already taken steps regarding the general framework of action. This has been based on an examination of the practices of other market economy countries and, especially, on the conclusions drawn from the international meetings organised under the aegis of the Conference of European Statisticians.

Among the first steps taken, we would mention the reorganisation of our statistical body which has now become the National Commission for Statistics. That means, first of all, the acknowledgement of the growing role of statistics in the state. The draft Statistics Law has been already drawn up and submitted to Parliament. It stipulates, among other things, the coordinating role of the National Commission for Statistics in the national statistical system, its autonomy in establishing the means and methods of data collection, compilation and dissemination, as well as in defining statistical indicators, nomenclatures and classifications. The Law also deals with the means of protecting the confidentiality of individual data, access to administrative data sources and cooperation with other data collecting and processing bodies.

The basic strategy for developing the statistical system of Romania, approved by the Government, has the following objectives:

a) The critical examination of the present information system and design of a new system based on the principles of a market economy;
b) The development and rationalisation of the flow of statistical data;
c) The adoption of a new accounting system for enterprises and other social and economic units and the implementation of the SNA;
d) The adoption of the United Nations statistical classifications, nomenclatures and methodologies;
e) The extension of sample surveys;
f) The use of administrative records;
g) The multiplication and enrichment of statistical publications, surveys and analytic studies required for decision-making in government, as well as for keeping the general public better informed;
h) The acquisition of improved computing equipment and software;
i) The intensification of international cooperation in statistics.

The examination of the present information system showed its incompatibility with the needs of the transition to a market economy. The present system subordinates data collection to monitoring plan fulfilment. The statistical service was almost totally dedicated to collecting and processing data for the decision-making bodies so they could manage, in an extremely centralised manner, the resources, production, supply and demand in practically all fields of socio-economic life. The heavy and simplistic informational system developed for this purpose had plenty of indicators but lacked the elements required for modelling the economic system and studying financial flows and impacts on social life. Some fields of statistics were almost wholly ignored: environment, economic efficiency, unemployment, inflation, business-cycle indicators, levels of living, legal statistics, etc.

The data collecting system was exclusively based on exhaustive surveys. Data were processed with obsolete computing equipment. Dissemination was restricted as confidentiality rules were applied even to aggregated data, and not just to individual records. In addition, there was a lack of public credibility, often justified, in statistical information.

In redesigning the statistical information system, there appear to be two alternatives. First, in view of Romania's decision to move to an open market economy, we could adopt a shock-therapy approach and try to implement, without reserve, the statistical methods and systems used by the traditional market economies. We do not regard this option as feasible from the practical point of view because we do not have the human and other resources that would be necessary. Apart from this, it would also be undesirable to make such a complete break with the past.

Another alternative is to correct and adjust the present system, partially adapting it to that of the market economy countries, particularly through conversion keys, adoption of complementary indicators, UN nomenclatures and classifications. Although this solution would cause less disturbance, it would not be suitable if it lasts too long, because that would lead to uncertainty and ambiguity for an indefinite period of time. It would also overwhelm our statistical service with demands for relevant information on important developments on new financial flows and other effects of the move towards a market economy.

As far as we are concerned, in this first transition stage, we would opt for a mixed solution. In concrete terms, that would imply:

- Clearing the ballast of indicators specific to the centralised planned economy, such as statistics on plan fulfilment and on execution of production and delivery contracts between enterprises.
- Maintaining, but revising, the system of physical indicators. Harmonising these with the respective indicators of the market economy countries seems to be much easier, as compared with value indicators.
- Continuing to compute the basic indicators of the Material Production System (MPS) for another 2-3 years. That will be useful for obtaining data which can be compared with past information, and will let us characterise the economic evolution during the transition period. We can also "translate" the MPS series into the System of National Accounts (SNA).
- Gradually introducing the SNA which, after a 2-3 year period, will become the main accounting system.
- Identifying the convergent elements of those two systems in order to avoid parallelism and ensure translation from one system to the other. This task could be more easily performed, if not even completely solved, through the studies, comparisons and solutions worked out by various international bodies (Conference of European Statisticians, CMEA, EEC, IMF, BIRD, OECD, etc.).

Against this background, the priority attached to implementing the national accounts system is obvious, since it should play a coordinating role for all economic statistics, and, to some extent, for demographic and social statistics too.

The development of national accounting requires a wide range of statistical information, including statistics on the administrative, financial and fiscal sectors. In this respect, the Ministry of Finance is now reorganising the bookkeeping practices of enterprises to bring them into line with market economy requirements. We would mention that, when the Law was passed regarding the setting up of private enterprises, a system for reporting the financial aspects of their activities was also created. This involves quarterly accounts covering income, expenses, profits and assets. The coverage of these accounts will be extended to meet the requirements of the national accounts system.

As regards economic statistics, important changes will be introduced so as to better meet users' needs. The system will be changed from one based on production and supply to one guided by demand. In this respect, the present system must be adapted so as to meet the requirement of measuring the level and structure of demand. We must also point out the importance of financial indicators, which were almost ignored in the past, or at least isolated from economic indicators.

Demographic and social statistics mainly refer to physical indicators, and fewer changes are required. In this field, we can find many convergent elements between the systems practised in the market economy countries and Central and Eastern European countries. We would, however, mention that some phenomena have not been sufficiently investigated: labour force supply and demand, unemployment, life quality and living standards according to social groups, environment, recreation and leisure time, tourism, cost of living and inflation, wages and salaries, etc.

Another priority field is statistics of prices. In this respect, we have to change the present method of collecting prices and define suitable price indices for measuring inflation. We must also point out that in passing to a private market economy, the fixed assets of all Romanian economic units will have to be revalued. Undoubtedly, that implies an adequate mechanism for revaluation and prices statistics will obviously play an important part here.

A really important and basic requirement is the redesigning of our data collection system. At present, the data collection system is based on the concomitant functioning of two channels:

a) enterprise → ministry → central statistical body; and
b) enterprise → territorial statistical unit → central statistical body.

In view of the planned decentralisation of the economy, we will try to find the optimal system of data collection, which should offer quality and timelines, cut down the information cost and avoiding duplication.

At the same time, with the enlargement of the private sector we are facing new problems never encountered in the past – namely non-response from economic and social units. As a preventive measure, we are trying to ensure that the Statistics Law on statistical enquiries will stipulate their compulsory nature. We have in mind to also use other methods of stimulating the units to provide data such as developing a "feedback" relation and offering them statistical information and publications in which they are interested. Better knowledge of other countries' practices in this field would be of a real benefit for us.

Data collection on an exhaustive (or "census") basis will not be possible under the new conditions. In this respect, great importance will be paid to sample surveys. Modern sampling techniques can provide data of acceptable reliability covering only limited numbers of small and medium-sized units. Such methods are widely practised in market economy countries and we need the assistance of specialists in this field.

For the implementation of the SNA, we intend to harmonise all data sources, including the administrative and tax data, and to use international concepts, definitions and terminology as much as possible. Implementation of the national accounts requires the adoption of classifications and nomenclatures used by international bodies such as the UN, OECD and EUROSTAT.

To achieve our objectives we have some general and some specific requests which we address to the international community. First the general:

a) We need documentation on the theory and practice of statistics compiled by the market economy countries.
b) The international organisations should work together to produce standard methodologies for compiling key economic, demographic and social statistics.
c) The international organisations should agree on a standard set of indicators. Methods for compiling them should also be made available.

Turning to specific request, our most pressing needs are for:

a) Technical assistance for the implementation of advanced statistics, specific to the market economy countries; paying expenses for our specialists during training periods in different countries.

b) Fellowships for young Romanian specialist for periods of three to six months.

c) Methodological papers, including questionnaires for data collection, tutorials for organising sample surveys, for organising and updating business registers, classifications, nomenclatures, publications, etc.

d) Participation by foreign specialists in the development of sample surveys using experience gained in their own countries.

e) Allocation of funds for the development of bilateral comparisons – i.e. purchasing power parities studies between our country and a market economy country.

f) Material support in supplying hardware and software for statistical data processing.

As far as we are concerned, we are completely open to multilateral cooperation and we believe that statistics is a fertile, useful and generous field for cooperation. We think that a goodwill attitude, without restrictions, and with equal treatment towards all transition countries should be the basic principles underlying the support provided by Western countries. Our targets imply many efforts and we are prepared to face them, but the material and financial difficulties are the most serious of all.

Adapting to Users Needs: the Experience of Statistics Sweden

Jüri Kôll
Statistics Sweden

Statistics Sweden has broadened its original mandate of providing statistics solely for government and now caters for a wide range of users. Special surveys are undertaken for interested users on a commercial basis and special tabulations and analyses of existing data are also provided. Emphasis on meeting market demands not only ensures that Statistics Sweden remains responsive to users' needs but also makes enterprises more willing to fill in questionnaires.

Introduction

With its origins in the "Statistical Tables Office" founded in 1749, Statistics Sweden is one of the oldest public authorities in Sweden and a forerunner to many statistical offices all over the world.

The task of Statistics Sweden, as of official statistical offices in other democratic countries, is to monitor those aspects of socio-economic development which are amenable to quantitative measurements. Historically, the statistics were mainly calculated to meet the needs of the government, but gradually the task has expanded.

From time to time, there are discussions about the role of Statistics Sweden. The question is whether Statistics Sweden should, as it previously did, render information services only or at least mainly to the government,or whether Statistics Sweden should become a major information supplier in the Swedish information society, and render information services to all types of agents in democratic and market economic processes.

The objective of Statistics Sweden

Today we clearly adhere to the latter position. Consequently the objective of Statistics Sweden can be formulated as the ambition to serve the following categories of users in the manner indicated:

a) The general public and their elected representatives in local councils as well as in the national Parliament are, through newspapers, television, libraries or other means, to have access to correct and relevant statistics concerning the present status and trends of different socio-economic phenomena in the Swedish society.

b) For economic, social, medical or other research, the official statistics are to provide an infrastructure, furthering the growth of knowledge. By this type of use, the statistical system is tested and developed by qualified users.

c) The Cabinet and the central government authorities are to be assisted in their evaluation and decision-making work in different policy areas by timely and accurate statistical data.

d) Local government bodies are to be provided with the statistics they need for estimation, evaluation and decision-making on their respective levels. As far as possible, these statistics for the different municipalities and counties are to permit the social conditions in different parts of the country to be compared.

e) The political parties, trade unions and other organisations are to have access to statistics that will assist them in formulating their respective standpoints.

f) The business community is to be provided with statistics than can reduce uncertainty in investment, price-setting, locational and other decisions.

g) The international society is to be provided with internationally comparable statistics according to internationally agreed classifications and guidelines.

The statistics we produce today naturally reflect the fact that, historically, they have been commissioned and financed by the government and the Parliament. Other users of statistics have not, as yet, similar facilities for commissioning and financing statistics. Or at least their possibilities do not equal the possibilities of the government and the Parliament.

Parallel to the change in the formulation of objectives, the process of producing statistics and of mapping user needs has changed. Statistics Sweden produces a very wide range of statistics, but this paper focuses on how we map the users' needs for economic statistics in Sweden, how we make the decisions on which economic statistics to produce, and how we organise production in order to retain a high degree of flexibility. Flexibility is an essential characteristic. Without it, we would not be able to meet the data needs we encounter.

Mapping user needs

As with any goods and services, demand for a statistical product only arises when there seems to be a reasonable chance of getting it. Similarly, good statistics can only be produced when the producer has some knowledge of how user will apply the statistics in their work. In other words, data needs can only arise and be identified in very close cooperation between the user and the producer. Without such cooperation, data needs cannot be mapped, nor can they be accommodated. Close cooperation means that the producer knows how the user works, the object of his work, the kind of analyses or decisions he has to make, the degree of certainty he needs in separate items of information and the time limits inherent in the work. The user, on his side, should understand the kinds of statistics it is possible to produce, the degree of certainty that can be attained, the periods for which data can be collected and the timeliness it is reasonable to expect.

There are several roads to cooperation. The first step must always be a high degree of willingness from the statistical office to try to solve the problems of all kinds of users. A meaningful dialogue can only develop when the users know that it is useful to discuss their problems with the statistical office.

During the seventies and eighties, Statistics Sweden announced in words and deeds its willingness to try to solve various information problems. The staff was taught how to respond to users and their requests and was motivated to give better service. Units were established to serve different kinds of users. A typical example is the Section for Regional Statistics, which was established to meet in particular the needs of regional planners, but which also serves all other users of regional statistics. A regional database was constructed, offering all kinds of statistics with relevant regional breakdowns.

Statistics Sweden also promotes cooperation by giving the staff opportunity to practice in the offices of various users. Still another way is to permit the staff of some users to work at Statistics Sweden.

Statistics Sweden staff quite often move on to employment with users of statistics. This has become a principal means of enhancing user cooperation. When members of the staff leave Statistics Sweden, they bring with them a good knowledge of how statistics are produced and they also bring with them (hopefully) good and easy relations with their previous colleagues. Personal contacts play a very important role in all kinds of cooperation. So, though we might regret the loss of competent staff, colleagues moving on (in manageable quantities) to become users of statistics have some positive effects for Statistics Sweden.

Finally, of course, our staff works together with statistics users in user groups initiated by Statistics Sweden, other working groups, government committees, research groups and so on.

Range of services offered

The services we offer are all linked to the production of statistics. The production process covers collection of data, compilation of statistics, maintenance of registers, analysis and distribution. In these areas we render services to everyone who is willing and able to pay the costs. One-fourth of our activities are paid for directly by the users, while three-fourths are paid for out of the government budget. Of the services directly paid for, reprocessing of already collected data constitutes the main part.

The planning process

Every third year, the planning process at Statistics Sweden requires us to discuss the plans for the coming three-year period with the main users of statistics. The discussions, as well as the planning, cover some forty statistical programmes. For each programme, the statistician in charge must discuss with all the main users of the programme in order to ensure that the programme proposed for the next three years meets the current needs of users. Parliamentary decisions on funds for statistics are based on these updated programmes.

The way this work is organised is partly a matter of circumstance. Some of the programmes are very wide and have a large number of users, while others are very specific and have only a few users. Each programme decides independently how to contact its users.

The most extensive programme is that of economic statistics for macro-economic policy. To get the views of its users in 1989, an "Economic Statistics Day" was organised. Its aim was to present plans for economic statistics and closely linked programmes to a broad group of users. A preliminary programme, based on the views of the biggest users of economic, industrial, credit market, transport, tourism and energy statistics, were sent to the almost one hundred users who had accepted the invitation. During the Day, everyone had the opportunity to comment on the preliminary programmes and to ask questions. The users included representatives of ministries, central and local government agencies, trade unions, employer and industry organisations, news-media and financial and non-financial enterprises.

The Economic Statistics Day was a success and brought Statistics Sweden a lot of good-will. Some other programmes have used the same approach, and we plan to continue these fairly elaborate gatherings of users.

Courses and seminars

To improve the knowledge of our statistical products among users, we also offer occasional courses on national accounts, financial accounts, indices and some other products. Besides a transfer of knowledge, these courses provide a good opportunity to establish personal contacts with the users.

The same can be said about our seminars with researchers and other users in the course of developing new statistical products or improving existing ones. During the last few years, we have held seminars on the hidden economy, service statistics, national accounts, credit market statistics, etc.

Priority setting

Priority setting is always a difficult problem, and economic statistics include elements that make it even worse. For instance, to give an up-to-date picture of the rapidly changing Swedish economy, we need at practically every planning period to include several new items of information. But because of the wide use of time-series in analyses, the value of new information is less than that of ongoing series. As a result, every time new data are introduced in place of old ones, the statistician has a very hard time to convince users. And it is the users who indicate the priorities.

The conflict between the users of time-series and the need for new survey questions, new classifications (the revision of the ISIC and the national activity classifications will spoil a lot of time-series) and new or modified entities, is an everlasting one. The problem becomes particularly acute in times of budget restraint, when it is out of the question to maintain all the old series at the same time that the new ones are being introduced.

Statistics Sweden tries to reduce the conflict in two ways. One is by linking time-series and thus making the effects of changes less severe for the users. The other is to organise discussions between the users of old time-series and the users who need information on new phenomena. In this way we hope to gain at least a grudging understanding of necessary modifications.

The final decision about whether some new statistics are to be produced is made by the Parliament if the statistics are to be funded from the government budget. In other cases it is made by the party commissioning the statistics. In the latter case, Statistics Sweden always reserves the right to publish the results if the statistics are of general interest. A paragraph in the contract gives Statistics Sweden the right to publish the results if the commissioning party chooses not to do so.

There are several cases of series started on the initiative of Statistics Sweden without very active support of users, which after some years have become widely used and highly supported by many users. This indicates that in areas where our statisticians are familiar with the analyses made by the users, they are able to foresee the use of new series at an earlier stage than the users themselves.

Government budget versus commercial funding

In 1987, the production of all credit-market statistics was put on a commercial basis. The final decision about which credit-market statistics to produce was transferred from government and Parliament to the users.

Statistics Sweden has noted that since 1987 when the users of the credit-market statistics, headed by the Swedish Bank Board, took over the financing and commissioning role, lack of funds is no longer the main restriction in modernising credit-market statistics for Sweden. The users seem more ready to accept changes and are more willing to pay for higher quality, when they themselves are paying for the statistics.

The extensive changes to the Swedish credit-market during the eighties as a consequence of a series of deregulation measures, will continue into the nineties and corresponding changes in the statistics will become necessary.

This experience triggered off a discussion as to whether other types of statistics should be put on a commercial basis as well. However, the multiple use of most economic statistics makes it difficult to find coherent groups of big users.

New statistics

When a survey is not financed from the government budget, a user or group of users have the possibility of financing it themselves and in that way get the information they desire. Some regular statistics have begun as ad-hoc surveys produced for the account of some specific user. A not uncommon way to get new statistics started is that a government committee proposes and finances one or two rounds of a survey. Its idea is primarily to check if the survey method will provide data of acceptable quality. As figures from two or three rounds give much more information about the phenomena in question than figures from just one round, the government may easily slip into funding the survey regularly.

Pattern of changes in economic statistics

Some of our economic statistics, e.g. financial statistics of local government, manufacturing statistics and foreign trade statistics, are very old. A lot of structural annual economic statistics were started in the fifties and sixties, e.g. enterprise finance statistics and most credit-market statistics. In the seventies, supplementary short-term statistics appeared and gaps in economic statistics begun to be filled in. But during the seventies, budget constraints began to affect statistics as well, and for some fifteen years we have had continuous budget cuts. In 1990, however, we got an increase in the funds for economic statistics, perhaps due to our users' complaints over the insufficient quality of some of the economic statistics.

During the long period of budget restraint we nevertheless managed to build up most of our service-industry statistics, improve the national accounts and start statistics on investments in marketing, software and research and development. We also had to balance new statistics against old ones, and some, like the statistics on expected imports, had to be discontinued. But because practically all economic statistics are used in the compilation of the national accounts, very few surveys were entirely suspended. Parts not necessary in the compilation of the national accounts were cut out, and the number of printed publications was reduced. At the same time, custom-made products paid for by the user increased very rapidly, so the total use of economic statistics increased considerably. Most of our users are in favour of the changes we have made, as these facilitate the production of statistics tailored to the specific needs of each user. General publications can never meet demands in the same way.

A flexible production system

Sometimes a demand for new statistical information can be met by restructuring data which has already been collected or by new combinations of available data. With a flexible production system, it is often relatively cheap to produce new information from available basic data.

In a flexible production system, micro-data ought to be stored in such a way that new classification systems can easily be used for aggregation. Particular details collected in separate surveys for the same entity ought to be stored with the same entity identifier.

Some examples of innovative applications are provided by enterprise statistics. These cover profit and loss and balance sheet data, as well as some supplementary information. The main results are estimates for aggregated activity classes according to the Swedish activity classification. Codes for ownership and legal form permit aggregations by enterprise group (corporation) and by legal form:

a) Aggregation by enterprise group yields the total activity of the group in Sweden. By using separately collected information on transactions inside the enterprise group and the totals for the entire group, Statistics Sweden can calculate, as a residual, totals for the group's activities abroad.

b) By using the codes of legal form, we have been able to test the effect of proposed new enterprise tax-rates and rules on the profit figures collected on financial statistics.

c) With information from an enterprise about its main competitors on the market, we can provide key-ratios (profit/turnover, profit/capital, etc.) for each enterprise in comparison with the median and quartile values for the group of enterprises it considers as its main competitors. (The group must include at least 10 enterprises.)

Coordinated statistics on economics

The coordination of concepts and classifications in economic statistics is based on the use of a common enterprise register as the sampling frame. All economic statistics at Statistics Sweden have to use the classifications of the enterprise register, both for enterprises and establishments. With the same activity, size groups and other classifications, and with the same unique identifier for each enterprise/establishment in all the surveys, it becomes possible to combine the results of the various surveys. Furthermore, the samples for the various annual and short-term surveys are coordinated as well.

The reference framework for all the Swedish economic statistics is the System of National Accounts (SNA). All published statistics are to link up to the relevant figure in the national accounts. We are not yet able to publish such links for all our statistics, but we hope to be able to do so at the end of this year.

Concluding remarks

Historically, Statistics Sweden has been a government body, compiling statistics mainly for the government and publishing statistics in general statistical publications. Today, the offices sees itself as an information agency working with all kinds of statistical information for the whole Swedish society. The users include the general public, enterprises, local government bodies and many others. This signifies an expanded use of statistics as a basis for decision and evaluations. To have individuals, private enterprises and other entities as users makes it easier, in turn, for us to collect figures for our statistics from those entities.

Freeing Resources for New Work: Statistics that can be Reduced or Phased out

Jaroslav Jilek
Federal Statistical Office,
Czech and Slovak Federal Republic

Statistical agencies in all Central and Eastern European countries are aware that they will have to radically improve many of the statistics that they now produce and introduce completely new types of data. Given tight budgetary restraints, it is clear that existing statistical programmes will have to be cut back to make room for new ones. This paper identifies statistics that could be reduced or phased out in the Czech and Slovak Federal Republic. Essentially these are statistics that were developed to monitor the execution of the central plan. It seems likely that similar kinds of statistics could be phased out in other Central and Eastern European countries.

Background

At the present time, the Federal Statistical Office of the Czech and Slovak Federal Republic is transforming the direction of its activities. The main reasons for this are the transition of society from totalitarianism to democracy and the transition to a federal system of government. While the discussions on the ways and the speed of these transformations have not yet been concluded, it is apparent that their implementation will take several years even according to the most radical proposals. Official statistics – the collection, processing, evaluation and presentation of numerical information on the state and on the development of socio-economic phenomena – have to respect the direction and speed of changes in society and in the national economy. If mistakes and unnecessary waste are to be avoided, it is important to distinguish between activities proper to official statistics in all developed countries and those that are directly linked to central planning. It will then be possible to determine when activities not corresponding to the nature of a market economy can be abolished, in line with the gradual withdrawal by the administration from the outdated practice of centralised management.

Statistics on reporting units' "economic plans"

The primary task of statistics in a centrally-planned economy is to check the fulfilment of the state plan. In the CSFR, the number of imperative indicators has been reduced already and the remaining ones are only of a guiding or informative nature. At the present time, one can say that the statistics do not deal with the fulfilment of the state plan; *the statistics are not used to compare actual and planned outcomes for individual reporting units and their various groupings.* Instead they are used to make comparisons of aggregates for industries and/or the national economy. The most significant comparisons are considered to be those comparing the actual outturn in the current period with the same period in the previous year (after any necessary corrections for differences in the number of work days). In the last few years, the imperative yearly targets of the state plan that were specified to reporting units included the creation of reserves. This has disturbed the seasonal patterns of production, and at present, *statistics on the total of the economic plans of reporting units are no longer compiled.* The only comparisons now made are of actual out-turns with the figures included in the state plan, usually disaggregated by ministries or by industries.

Detailed supply/demand balances for commodities

A cardinal feature of a centrally-planned economy is an insufficient supply of goods and services to meet the effective demand. Starting from the planned balances, statistics are compiled aimed at characterising the generation of resources and their distribution and use. These statistics show the supply/demand balances for individual kinds of raw and processed materials, energy, investment goods and consumer goods as well as balances for aggregates such as the generation and use of the social product and national income. Unfortunately, a common feature of these balances is they cannot be used to derive either the level or relative significance of unsatisfied demand; these can only be estimated indirectly and approximately using changes in stock levels (the state material reserves included). *The compilation of individual balances will be gradually abolished* with balances for the most important types of raw material being the last to go. This will involve a gradual reduction in the statistics of the so-called "material-supply" system – or the "supplier-user" relationship.

Sales statistics

So-called "sales statistics" will also be reduced. These statistics refer to sales of own-produced and purchased goods and they presently make distinctions between sales for investment (including own investment), for exports (split into socialist and non-socialist countries) and for internal trade. Sales for exports are valued at both domestic and foreign prices and the sales for internal trade at both wholesale and retail prices (double pricing). *The classification of sales by planning groups – i.e., by groups of organisations with approximately the same production programmes* will be dropped. It is also likely that *the classification of sales by about 500 production branches will be abandoned.* A similar breakdown of own production of reporting units will, however, still be available.

Labour balances

The balances of labour sources and their distribution have also been compiled for these same individual balances. Labour sources include people of working age, those who are employed but are over working age plus employed foreigners; the distribution of manpower includes persons as described above, persons preparing for their profession such as students and apprentices, disabled persons, and persons not working. *Yearly instead of quarterly labour balances are now considered to be adequate*, but a more detailed breakdown of unemployed persons will be called for with special attention to those looking for jobs. On a monthly basis, the numbers of persons employed, persons looking for jobs and persons re-trained after their loss of job will be surveyed.

The social product and the sources and uses of national income only refer to the so-called productive sphere, i.e., activities which result in the materialisation of goods; the so-called non-productive sphere is treated separately. It is expected that as long as the CMEA exists or as long as the CSFR remains a member of the CMEA, it will be desirable to go on compiling indicators corresponding to the MPS. The balances in the MPS contain indicators of both created and utilised social product and national income together with their basic components. By 1st January 1992, statistics on the gross and net domestic and national products will be compiled. These data will have a broader coverage than those on the "produced national income" according to the MPS. From then on, national accounts of Classes 1, 2 and 3 will be compiled according to the 1968 SNA. In connection with the transition from the MPS to the SNA, *the distinction between so-called "productive" and "non-productive" activities will not be applied as rigorously as it has been so far.* This will reduce the demands made on reporting units. It should also be added that internal enterprise accounting will be simplified by allowing enterprises to classify internal or "ancillary" units according to the main activity of the enterprise.

Indicators of gross output

The backbone of the national economic plan in a centrally-planned economy is assigning the quantities of products to be made and allocating their subsequent distribution and use. As a result, indicators of gross output have a priority position. However, the gross output boundary is dependent on the definition adopted for finished production; for example, the production volume from the viewpoint of the establishments of a given enterprise will exceed that from the viewpoint of the enterprise as a whole if there is intra-enterprise cooperation in production. In addition to measuring production on an enterprise basis, the CSFR statistics were also compiled on the basis of "product", "branch" (defined according to the production classification), "establishment" and "concern". These different bases were imposed for various purposes and varied from one industry to another. In future, the indicators of gross output are expected to become of secondary significance only, and the method of computing them will be determined by the way in which it is decided to compute value added. *This means that reporting units will no longer have to compute either planned or actual indicators of gross output in comparable prices according to the obligatory methodology.* In the past, these data were used to derive the indices of physical production volumes and the indicators of "fulfilment of planned quantities of production". It also means, however, that a new method of computing the indices of industrial, agricultural and construction output will have to be introduced. This will be based on representative products.

The emphasis laid on the full coverage of physical production is also reflected in a variety of other production indicators: besides the indicators of gross output, which also cover changes in stocks and work in progress, indicators excluding these changes were also called for. There were also indicators of commodity ouptut for industrial activities, indicators of market production for agriculture, which excluded agricultural output used for intermediate consumption in agriculture, and indicators of sales of both own-produced and contracted-out construction outputs. Furthermore, the above-mentioned indicator of sales (own and purchased outputs) was surveyed for both industrial and sales organisations. Obviously, the *variety of the above indicators, is unnecessarily broad*, and it will suffice, in future, to restrict measurement to indicators of deliveries, together with gross output statistics needed for calculating value added in manufacturing.

The above mentioned output indicators for individual industries are related to establishment statistics. However, in calculating the national income of the CSFR, the so-called output indicators of organisations are relied on, and they can also be referred to as indicators of gross output. Using these indicators, *both a detailed breakdown of output and the composition of costs associated with that output were surveyed. It is intended to reduce the amount of detail*, but the possibility of computing the net material product according to the MPS and value added according to the SNA will have to be maintained.

Profit indicators

While great importance was attached to quantity or "physical volume" indicators, the other side of the coin was that profit indicators were largely ignored. This stemmed from the fact that the relative prices of individual kinds of goods not only failed to correspond with the demand/supply relation, but also frequently ignored relations among the amounts of production factors used to produce the different goods. For this reason profit indicators could express neither the benefit to society resulting from a given activity nor the significance of changes when different production factors are utilised. As a result the following indicators were introduced and followed at virtually all levels of management:

- Indicators of economy in the consumption of selected kinds of raw materials, energy and all inputs. These were measured as differences between the so-called "specific consumption indicators" and the cost ratio, with specific consumption being understood as consumption per specified unit of output.
- Indicators of labour utilisation intensity. These included not only indicators of labour productivity (usually measured inaccurately by reference to gross output), but also indicators of working time, indicators of the number of workers appointed and dismissed, etc.
- Indicators of the intensity of utilisation of building and production equipment. These included indicators of equipment operation time, the so-called

shift rate indicators, shares of gross output per unit of equipment at acquisition value, etc. (It is worth mentioning that no utilisation of production capacity was kept under review except for power plants and some machinery.)

A substantial number of the indicators above is expected not to be statistically surveyed any longer, as the function of profit will be restored under market conditions, and decisions on the utilisation of production factors will be made by the economic agents themselves and not by management bodies at a supra-enterprise level. At the national level there will continue to be interest in the indicators of labour productivity (using value added for the calculation, however), average length of work day/week, overall cost ratios or profit to cost ratios and capacity utilisation indicators.

Research and development statistics

As the profit indicators could not respond to changing relations between supply and demand, they were almost entirely insensitive to benefits from the implementation of research and development (R&D) findings. This was the main reason for establishing R&D statistics. Benefits from research and development projects were poorly estimated due to imperfect benefits resulting from R&D. The aggregate net benefit for the national economy were then clearly over-estimated and, consequently, often exceeded the overall annual increase in the national income (with the amount of labour rising). These statistics could not be taken seriously and this led to further deterioration in the quality of these statistics.

In future these statistics will not be designed to keep track of the progress of individual research and development projects, except for those financed from public budgets. It is further intended that *the indicators characterising the implementation of R&D projects will be reduced in number* with priority being given to those projects that are directed at the acquisition of new technology rather than to those aimed at new products based on existing technologies.

Statistics on inventories

The systematic excess of demand over supply meant that holding excessive production stocks (of both raw materials and semi-finished products) was an advantage from the point of view of enterprises rather than a disadvantage, because the higher interest payments due on the stocks, for which credit was anyway granted by the State Bank, did not usually affect profits to any significant extent. This was the reason for introducing indicators of rate of stock turnover (turnover time in particular) as well as indicators of unnecessary and surplus stock volumes. These data were aggregated at various levels up to that of the national economy. *The indicators of turnover time of stocks are expected to become enterprise indicators only and the statistical surveying of surplus and unnecessary stocks will be abandoned.* However, levels of stocks of goods for sale will become of priority interest and will be surveyed quarterly at first and then on a monthly basis.

Capital asset statistics

Modernisation of the machinery belonging to individual reporting units was rarely linked to the profit that the units earned. However, statistics on investment and on fixed assets, i.e., buildings, machinery, equipment, means of transport and the like, were very thorough (perhaps the most perfect among the ex-socialist countries) as they were used for central decision-making on the location of investment projects.

The statistics of fixed assets, which are kept in an automated manner, use both original cost price and residual cost values and are classified by type of asset, by age structure, by the nature of output and by type of organisation. The indicators are updated *every year. These statistics are supposed to be brought up to date with the censuses of industry* performed every five years and some of the surveyed indicators are going to be changed. In particular, assets will be valued at current replacement costs.

The investment statistics also included the so-called "register of construction projects" which was also computerised. In 1989, the register covered over 100 indicators characterising each of 4 000 projects, each with an expected value of over 10 million Kcs. Although the register was founded in 1971, the necessary completeness of data on the projects has not been achieved and no rational way of using the data has been devised. In fact, the location of investment projects was primarily decided on political grounds which is why the explanations of economic results in the operation of individual projects were generally unconvincing, no matter how ingenious the explanations may have been. As a result, *the register of construction projects in its present form will not be kept any longer.* Consideration is being given to the registration of all construction permits; this may not be done in a centralised manner, however, due to the federal arrangement of the state.

Input-output tables

The relative prices of individual kinds of goods in the CSFR resulted from the planned management of prices. A significant instrument for planning wholesale prices (of industrial, construction and agricultural production) was the input-output tables compiled every five years – the latest referring to 1987. These tables included commodity balances for nearly 500 branches, i.e., aggregations of goods or services in compliance with the CSFR classifications of industrial, construction, agricultural and forest outputs as well as transport, communications and trade. The use of imported goods and services was reported separately from that of domestic production using two kind of valuation – producers' prices or final-use prices. To eliminate the consequences of frequent changes in organisation, the production of industry was judged according to the branch method i.e., each product that acquired characteristics corresponding to the product branch title was assigned to that branch.

The input-output tables were compiled from data collected by periodic surveys which were very extensive and time-consuming for reporting units; for each product branch, the structure of costs incurred was surveyed in each organisation, the material consumption also being split into 500 items and the consumption of imports being reported separately. In future, *the input-output tables will be compiled by combining make and use matrices* using the procedure recommended for the SNA (Rev.3) and the tables are very likely to be classified in accordance with the ISIC divisions. This should substantially reduce the amount of work and the costs involved in their compilation. It is expected that these tables will be used in long-term planning.

Distinction between "productive" and "non-productive" spheres

Making a distinction between "productive" and "non-productive" spheres was administratively very demanding not only for reporting units, which had to distinguish between the two spheres in their intra-enterprise accounting, but also for the Federal Statistical Office itself, especially in computing the "produced national income". Most organisations in the CSFR are large and, therefore, engage in activities spread over many industries. With these large organisations, producing units belonging to different industries delivered their output to other units within the organisation; in other words, intermediate consumption was created among various industries in this way. If the structure of the value of outputs that were intended for external users was to be calculated correctly, it was necessary to compile a kind of input-output table for each enterprise (with all industry-industry relations within a given enterprise included in Quadrant I) and to calculate the components of value added by manufacturing contained in the final product (classified by industries) of each individual enterprise. The calculations were time-consuming and cost-intensive, though they were made in an automated manner. *It is expected that this elaborate method will be applied, for the last time, to calculations of the 1991 produced national income in the sphere of production.* Henceforth, establishment statistics, including the associated concept of "ancillary activity", will be used.

Sample surveys versus complete coverage

The statistical supervision over the fulfilment of the state plan had to be comprehensive and, therefore, the room for application of sample surveys was small. Sample surveys are expected to be first used in obtaining indicators for business cycle analysis. *The monthly exhaustive surveying of the volumes of industrial and construction outputs is being abandoned* and will be replaced by the calculations of indices of industrial and construction outputs using volume indices of representative products. Indices of wholesale and retail prices will continue to be based on the prices of representative products. However, these prices will be surveyed as of the 15th day of each month and will not be calculated as weighted arithmetic means from quarterly data on the volumes and values of goods sold.

The prerequisite for establishing a rational system of sample surveys is the existence of a reliable base for selection. That is why a register of surveying units is going to be established and the register should permit the creation of sets of units of both enterprise and establishment types. The existing register of organisations, which presently covers legal subjects engaged in economic activities, will be used as a basis. On the other hand, the so-called registers of data carriers will be abolished; being 23 in number, they were special registers for reporting units of individual sector statistics. They could not be mutually connected, which was the basic cause why the same data was sometimes collected several times. (This situation was the consequence of direct dependence of the organisation of official statistics on the state planning bodies.)

Standard classifications

In 1948, when the communists took over, the CSFR belonged to the group of developed economies. Following the mechanical adoption of Soviet methods of management, planning and statistics (1951-1953), which ignored the stage of development achieved in the CSFR, the introduction of some divergent standards was permitted. This was especially the case with the standard system of socio-economic classifications introduced in the CSFR in the 1960s. Its fundamental feature is its uniqueness and it is necessary to convert its parts (classification of industries, classification of branches and products, classification of occupation and the like) not only to the classifications recommended by the UN (ISIC, SITC, HS, ISCO, etc.) but also to those recommended by the CMEA. *The standard system of socio-economic classifications of the CSFR is expected to be dropped*, and the system will be replaced by internationally employed classifications which may, in extreme cases, be modified to reflect special circumstances. It is assumed that the new classifications will, in principle, come into use along with the introduction of the SNA in the CSFR from 1st January 1992. By that time, however, appropriate methods of interfacing the old and new classifications will have to be found, so that the previous statistical series can be continued and so that reporting units can continue to supply data. The fact that reporting units are still obliged to employ some parts of the system of classifications (especially the classification of branches and products, standard classification of performance, standard classification of fixed assets and standard classification of occupation) in their intra-enterprise accounting cannot be ignored. In this connection it is worth mentioning that *the practice of statistical surveying, in which reporting units calculated hypothetical indicators (such as volumes of output produced and sold expressed in terms of constant prices) is being phased out*. Consequently, the way of keeping intra-enterprise accounting will not be directively assigned, either.

Concluding remarks

In summarising the intentions to get rid of the statistics linked to the previous practice of central planning in the CSFR, it should be noted that the idea is not to abolish any parts in their entirety, but rather to make partial changes. This stems both from the fact that the transition of the national economy to market conditions will be gradual (for the time being the CSFR is not going to sever its links with the CMEA) as well as from the fact that CSFR official statistics dealt with all areas of socio-economic phenomena even though sometimes in a "deformed" manner (if a market economy is considered as the norm). We believe that the transformation of the CSFR official statistics can be compared to the thinning of a young forest supplemented in part with new planting. Considered as fundamental are the introduction of internationally used classifications, adaptation of survey periodicity to the rhythm of economic cycles and wide application of sample survey methods. This implies dropping the CSFR system of socio-economic classifications, breaking the mechanical link with the practice of central economic planning and abandoning supervision over the activities of reporting units.

Last but not least, I should mention efforts which will have to be made by the CSFR official statisticians to gain public confidence in the results of their work. This means uprooting, from both statistical practice and awareness of the public, the "self-lying principle" by which official statisticians gladly accepted favourably exaggerated results from reporting units and the users of the statistics behaved as if they were objective, even though they themselves had frequently participated in "improving" them.

While the ideas presented in this paper are based on the intentions of the management of the Federal Statistical Office, their interpretation represents the author's personal views. This is not only because of the complex and close ties between the existing official statistics and the official statistics to come, but more particularly because of our uncertainty about how much time individual steps in the transformation of our economy and society will take.

IV

Special Topics

Supply and Suppliers of Data: Compulsion or Cooperation

Jacob Ryten
Statistics Canada

The paper describes the various measures by which Statistics Canada has achieved high rates of response to its business surveys. Particular importance is attached to winning the cooperation of respondents in spite of the fact that the Canadian Statistics Act makes compliance with all surveys compulsory. Questionnaires use the language of business and are confined as far as possible to information that businesses already collect for their own purposes. Response burdens are reduced by eliminating very small enterprises from surveys and by using tax-returns and company accounts in place of questionnaires. Statistics Canada's reputation for impartiality, political independence and data protection is also an important element in preserving the cooperation of respondents. Establishing and maintaining good relations with respondents is not costless and should be explicitly budgeted in drawing up survey programmes.

I. Introduction

The purpose of this paper is to convey the experience of the Canadian statistical agency vis-à-vis its respondents or, more generally, the constituencies from which data are gathered. It is mostly a descriptive paper. Its point is to suggest that even though there is a legal framework that allows the statistical agency to conduct mandatory surveys and that defines sanctions where respondents refuse or neglect to reply, in practice there is a complex cooperative network that took time to establish and is fairly expensive to maintain. But without this effort at securing cooperation, the effects on the quality of the data collected and published would be disastrous.

There was a visit, in 1990, by Statistics Canada to the Hungarian Central Statistical Office (HCSO). It was short but it was not the first contact between the two agencies. It served for the management of the HCSO to describe some of the new problems it faced as the Hungarian economy entered a stage of transition and to underscore the fact that whereas the number of actual and potential respondents for collection of business statistics was increasing rapidly, there were no good formal or informal means to identify them and to bring them into the circle of regular respondents to HCSO surveys. Nor were there established traditions and procedures that would allow the HCSO to decide what proportion of its resources should be allocated to this purpose. This is a simplification which doubtless glosses over a number of other factors but its point is to suggest that there was an acute problem, the nature of which was new and about which the fruits of relevant experience were being sought.

By extension we speculated that statistical offices in other economies in transition were bound to face similar problems and that it might be of assistance to provide them with an account of how these matter are dealt with in Canada, a country with a large and centralised statistical agency. Naturally, one ought not to assume that solutions to the problem of response and respondent relations are exportable with no change. After all, the problems arise in a particular institutional setting that owes much to the way in which government is looked upon, the understanding that respondents have of the need to collect and use statistical information, the confidence that they attach to the statistical agency, the willingness that exists to comply with government injunctions and so on. But even after allowing for national variations, we contend that there are elements in Canadian practice that could be adopted without much change and with a reasonable chance of success.

Note that the solutions that have been instituted by Statistics Canada to secure cooperation need not be adopted wholesale. They do reinforce each other, of course, but some at least can be effective even if adopted in isolation. The description provided in this paper is therefore in the nature of a menu from which to pick and choose. What is not available is a quantitative assessment of the relative efficacity of each of the measures that Statistics Canada has adopted. Its absence will have to be replaced by more or less inspired hunches.

II. Scope and background

The rest of the paper deals with response from business and relations with other government agencies. Of course, many of the issues upon which it touches apply to households and indeed some of the more delicate aspects of convincing respondents to comply relate to households. For example, cooperation by households may account for the difference between a good and an indifferent Census of Population. But since what is truly new in economies in transition is the rapid creation and demise of business enterprises and the fact that relations among the agencies of government are changing fast, we concentrate on them.

Statistics Canada, like so many other statistical agencies, was created by an Act of Parliament that defined its purpose and powers to collect data whether they be held by entities in the private sector or by other public agencies. This power is considerable. It allows, for example, access to tax information in the hands of the tax authorities just as much as to records kept by business for the purpose of running the business and which are germane to the purposes which Statistics Canada serves. Failure to comply with Statistics Canada's request for information may result in a fine or in a prison sentence or in both:

> "S29... Every person who, without lawful excuse, *(a)* refuses... to answer... any question... is... guilty of an offence and is liable on summary conviction to a fine not exceeding five hundred dollars or to imprisonment for a term not exceeding three months or to both." *Statistics Act, May 1981.*

Surveys undertaken by Statistics Canada are mandatory by law and ministerial dispensation must be obtained to make them voluntary.

On the strength of this Act, Statistics Canada conducts some 400 surveys and accesses "information holdings" in some 20 federal government departments. The number of business entities that are approached directly or indirectly is very large. Counting farms as businesses, the total number is of the order of one million. The nature of the contacts differs in length and medium. In some case businesses are approached by telephone and in others by mail; in some by interviewer and in others still, indirectly through their accounts or through some other government agency. At all times businesses can negotiate the submission of an alternative to a filled-in questionnaire. For example, the annual report to shareholders or the financial statement prepared for purposes of taxation is acceptable as a means to ease the business's burden. Some of the surveys are easy to comply with. They require three or four data items which typically are available from the business accounts department with no special calculations needed. Others are onerous. For example, there are surveys of regulated industries where compliance demands an investment of anywhere between ten and twenty hours.

The rates of response that Statistics Canada attains are high by most standards. For example, in the case of surveys of retailers, a category which is heavily dominated by small business not naturally disposed to comply with government requests, particularly when the value of such requests does not accrue to them directly, the rate of response for a monthly survey is well in excess of ninety per cent. Even in the case of some of the more complex surveys – of which the annual survey of manufacture is a good example – rates in the upper eighties are reached.

And yet, Statistics Canada throughout its history has very seldom resorted to its powers in order to enforce compliance. Indeed, since it is highly questionable whether any court would issue a prison sentence and since the fine that it could apply is by now almost nominal – certainly less than the cost of the work required to comply with the typical business questionnaire – resorting to judicial means would probably backfire and harm the rates of response that are now attained.

III. Methods and strategies

The question that follows from these considerations is an obvious one: granted that there is compliance and granted that the means to enforce it are weak and in any case seldom resorted to, to what does Statistics Canada owe its relative success?

The belief at Statistics Canada is that in order to secure compliance it must be perceived in a certain way by respondents. The following are elements which we think are essential to that perception. They are further developed in the next section:

a) The information solicited must be connected to an intelligible purpose to which businesses can relate;
b) The way in which the information is collected must show some understanding of how businesses keep their records;
c) The language used for collecting the information must be the language which is used for business to operate on a day to day basis;

d) The statistical agency must be seen as willing to accommodate respondents either by providing additional explanations or by accepting legitimate substitutes for a filled-in questionnaire;

e) The statistical agency must be perceived as thoughtful and concerned with response burden, that is to say that it is committed to finding means that will either simplify the burden imposed on business or exempt businesses from response outright;

f) The statistical agency must be perceived as holding in the strictest confidence all individual records submitted to it and not granting access to those records to anyone else in government or in the private sector; and

g) The professionalism and objectivity of the statistical agency, its freedom from political interference and its commitment not to extend preferential treatment to anyone or any body must be established, accepted and continually advertised.

There is an obvious means of coaxing unwilling respondents to reply to questionnaires. But Statistics Canada is not legally entitled to pay respondents for services rendered. There were marginal cases – for example, in the case of certain farm surveys Statistics Canada provided respondents with a copy of the Canada Yearbook or of a booklet of facts and figures on farming in Canada – but that is either no longer done or else it is on a scale so small that it can be ignored for purposes of this discussion.

IV. Approaches

a) The information solicited must be connected to an intelligible purpose to which businesses can relate.

b) The way in which the information is collected must show some understanding of the ways in which businesses keep their records.

c) The language used for collecting the information must be the language which is used for business to operate on a day to day basis.

Statistics Canada follows a set policy whenever it launches a survey. After having identified and selected respondents it approaches them, usually through its local office, with a letter that communicates in simple language why the survey is being conducted and to which extent failure to provide reliable information on the issue at hand could harm public discussion of what government should do about it.

Whenever Statistics Canada launches a business survey it attempts to enlist the cooperation and expert advice of the trade or industrial association that is connected with the survey's target population. In certain cases the system of consultation is elaborate. That has to do with the degree to which the particular business group is organised. In other cases it is informal. But in all cases, the purpose is to determine appropriate language, ascertain what are the forms of record-keeping, ensure that the results are meaningful, and the classifications adopted are understood and seen to be relevant to the business group that is being surveyed. Of course, this is a complex process particularly for large and continuing surveys. In fact, it implies that trade or industrial associations are involved in the planning of the survey. The upside of this is that they can also help with the management of public relations before the survey is introduced in order to maximise the goodwill with which it is received and the response rates which can be expected.

The matter of understandable language must not be played down. Statistics Canada has had for a long time a small technical group assigned to questionnaire design. But whereas this group was very active in matters relating to household questionnaires, less attention was paid to business surveys. This was an error which is now being rectified. Statistics Canada owes this initiative to the Australian Bureau of Statistics whose pioneering work in redrafting questionnaires in a language accessible to business people it gratefully acknowledges.

Even though the purpose for which the survey data are primarily collected may be well communicated to and accepted by business, Statistics Canada has found that it is a wise investment to provide as a by-product something that is of direct relevance to businesses irrespective of its size or geographic location. This is not usually possible with households except in very marginal cases. And even with business it is at times difficult. For example, it is of very little consequence to a small retailer or provider of consumer services whether or not the expenditure of consumers in the national accounts is reliably calculated. If surveys of retailers include esoteric requests for information such as classes of commodities sold, categories of customers to whom those commodities are sold, differences between new and second hand equipment goods sold, etc., all of which are obvious elements of information for national accounting purposes, the unwillingness to comply goes up markedly.

For this reason there has been experimentation with providing respondents directly with information which they can use for their own planning and management needs. For example, in the case of the quarterly survey of business conditions, respondents receive a table showing how their opinions and forecasts compare with the average for their industry. In the case of a new survey on the accuracy of short-term forecasts, forecasters are given a graph that locates their forecast in the range of forecasts received. And for the monthly surveys of retail and wholesale sales, the idea of providing each respondent with the current sales and inventories for their respective industry and region within Canada is being actively pursued.

The efficacity of these ideas has been indirectly tested. In Statistics Canada's programme of data for small business, one major source of demand comes from small business and is directed at the tables that show the key operating ratios (advertising to total expenses, sale space to total floor space, inventories to gross receipts, etc.) for their type of store and provides some information on failure rates for each portion of the distribution of the ratios.

d) The statistical agency must be seen to be willing to accommodate respondents either to provide additional explanations or to accept legitimate substitutes for a filled-in questionnaire.

e) The statistical agency must be perceived as thoughtful and concerned with response burden, that is to say that it is committed to finding means that will either simplify the burden imposed on business or exempt businesses from response outright.

It is a natural question for respondents to ask why their financial submission to the tax authorities or their annual report to stockholders – so long as it is audited – cannot be used in lieu of replies to lengthy and often cumbersome questionnaires. For a while, some of us deceived ourselves into thinking that just because our concepts were somewhat different from those specified and approved by the income tax laws, financial submissions for tax purposes could not be used. This form of conceit had two undesirable consequences: it irritated businesses because they could not understand the importance of subtle differences between national accounting and income tax standards (and, let us add, statisticians were not particularly good at explaining them) and because even when information was provided in reply to a questionnaire it was not possible to determine without a considerable investment of time and resources whether or not the information complied with statistical or taxation concepts.

For small and even medium-size businesses the chances are overwhelming that the firm's accounting departments – quite frequently a purchased service – are in no position to maintain two accounting systems. As an example, where the business has defined its fiscal year differently from the calendar year and where the questionnaire requests a calendar year adjustment, seldom can this be made with any degree of reliability. For these reasons, Statistics Canada decided that the most prudent policy was to accept existing statements where possible and concentrate its auditing resources for those large firms where the accounting department had the competence and indeed might have the incentive to provide adjusted estimates, but to allow all others to submit the best proxy they had (as long, of course, as the standards and conventions upon which the latter were based were well understood and documented).

This posture made it possible for Statistics Canada to capitalise on its unrestricted access to administrative documents including those produced for taxation purposes. Thus between 1978 and last year, the burden imposed by survey taking on businesses was reduced by almost two thirds. The measure of burden was calculated by computing on the basis of direct information the average time taken to reply to Survey A and multiplying that time by the number of actual respondents to the survey. The calculation is robust to the extent that for each survey the important number is the index which relates the current to the base period burden. And even though the nominal times required to reply to each survey are used as weights and reductions have not affected surveys uniformly, the results would not change substantially even if the weights were partly distorted.

Other measures that Statistics Canada has taken and is continuing to take in order to maintain a careful stance in imposing response burden is to design surveys in which panels of small businesses are periodically rotated out of the sample. Previously, a business once selected often got to complain that the selection became a life sentence. This view, once communicated to a trade association or worse still to a Parliamentarian and thereafter to the Minister Responsible for Statistics Canada's affairs could set off a wave of resistance to regular questionnaires.

Selecting those business that *a priori* are sufficiently small and simple in structure not to require any direct surveying, is probably best done if the criteria are made explicit and given publicity. In the case of Statistics Canada this was done in conjunction with the structure of its business list. Thresholds were defined for each industry-province combination – note that in Canada there is great variety in the size, population, and economic importance of each of its ten province – and it was announced to business that any unit below the appropriate threshold would not be surveyed at all or would not be surveyed directly for any of its financial results. All others however would, it being clear that in certain instances, questionnaire proxies would be acceptable.

In order to coordinate these multiple measure, Statistics Canada assigned a very senior official to look after all matters arising from relations with business respondents. These involve survey planning, questionnaire design, use of proxies, identification of contacts within the business, high level liaison with trade associations and so on.

Probably none of these measures in themselves is sufficient to create a general impression of thoughtfulness about introducing new burdens and of parsimony in terms of exploiting as much as possible data collected and data available through other means. Statistics Canada has still not reached one of its fundamental goals which is that of allocating burden with equity. Because hitherto the management of surveys beyond the stage of drawing samples from a central file was left to a great extent to the care of each survey-taking administration within Statistics Canada, equitable measures across surveys could not be taken. But with the advent of the newest version of the business register one of its applications is to measure how much burden has been imposed on a single business and so avoid overloading it with questionnaires.

The important point connected with this digression is that in Statistics Canada's experience, an effort must be made to be, and to be seen to be, thoughtful about response burden. To be seen thoughtful demands that measures of response burden be published periodically; that the body politic appears to take serious note of them; and that it encourage all those departments who make significant progress towards burden reduction. These conditions are necessary to impress upon business that new requirements are not likely to be frivolous or not thought through.

f) The statistical agency must be perceived as holding in the strictest confidence all individual records submitted to it and not granting access to those records to anyone else in government or in the private sector.

No amount of persuasion, thoughtfulness with response burden, provision of information designed to demonstrate the relevance and importance of a particular inquiry would suffice to persuade a business to cooperate if, at the same time, business was not convinced that whatever information they provide to Statistics Canada is subject to the strictest confidentiality. True, when asked in an abstract sense whether they believe that information that is held within one government department flows freely to others, the reply given by business is frequently "yes". But at the same time on countless occasions when a business had to choose to whom to give information, its choice was invariably the statistical agency on the grounds that it was the one that knew how to treat with confidentiality the records it received.

Confidentiality like any of the many attributes with which a statistical agency must be endowed takes a long time to build up and can be lost "in one afternoon". Statistics Canada has promoted the observance of confidentiality into a veritable cult not so much because of the need to go to extremes in an objective sense but because of the importance of perceptions. In particular, the statistical agency built up three principles. Firstly, what information goes in to it is secure. Names and addresses of individual reporters are only kept where it is essential and for as long as they are truly required. In this connection, visitors to Statistics Canada's buildings are subject to security screening. Secondly, there is no electronic access to data holdings from outside the building. Statistics Canada's computing is divided into two networks. The network through which confidential information (on individual businesses or households) flows is not accessible from anywhere outside the building complex that houses the agency. And lastly, there is considerable rigour in the confidentiality checks to which data are subjected before they are released to the public in case they allow disclosure of an individual respondent's characteristics. This last principle justifies the financing of researchers whose task is to improve the mathematical algorithms designed to test for open and residual disclosure of actual tabulations.

Statistics Canada maintains active cooperative links with the two tax revenue departments in the Canadian Federal government. The purposes are straightforward: in the case of Customs and Excise the relation is to support the acquisition of all records that have to do with foreign merchandise trade. And in the case of Taxation, it is mostly to obtain substitutes for all the information that Statistics Canada does not gather through direct surveying. There are at least two risks with such an association: firstly, its closeness can give rise to the suspicion on the part of respondents, and particularly business respondents, that the revenue department may be using Statistics Canada's expertise for audit and detection work not to mention using data that Statistics Canada has collected for other purposes and which when put together could provide a powerful auditing tool. The second is that the association is one-sided but sooner or later the department of Taxation will request a quid pro quo that, if satisfied, would push Statistics Canada across an invisible line between what is and what is not confidential information.

Hitherto, no such line was crossed and Statistics Canada has been open in its dealings with the public about the access that it gets to tax documents. Notwithstanding, it has insisted that the traffic is strictly one-sided and that it will not even return to the revenue agency documents which in the first instance were administrative but to which Statistics Canada may have added a code based on information gleaned from other sources. There is of course some tension as a result and the management of that relation is one of the major challenges for the leadership of the statistical office and one in which its most senior people are involved.

g) The professionalism and objectivity of the statistical agency, its freedom from political interference must be established, accepted and continually advertised.

Some ten years ago the Canadian Government created a civilian intelligence agency and vested in it full powers of access to other government department's data, documentation and generally speaking information holdings. There is only one exception to the powers of the agency – Statistics Canada. The matter was hotly debated as it is not immediately obvious whether in fact there ought to be exceptions in matters of national security. But in the end, the notion prevailed that the delicate fabric of relations between surveyors and surveyed and the objectivity that must permeate everything that the government's statistical agency says and does would be too rudely tested if its data collections were subject to the scrutiny of an intelligence agency. This means that if indeed there were a reason of national security that would demand inspection of Statistics Canada's individual data, Parliament would have to step in, modify the Statistics Act or have it replaced by new legislation.

The principle of non-interference in any of the agency's activities is cardinal to its role and to its relations with respondents. There are hundreds of thousands of contracts which use the Consumer Price Index or one of the Industrial Price Indexes as standards for settlement in the event of price change. Those contracts can only hold if the general public is persuaded of the agency's objectivity. Both the Federal Government and regional governments – or in Canadian parlance provincial governments – abide by income sharing formulae which are driven by current statistics – on gross provincial product, personal income, employment and unemployment, etc. There may be an argument to suggest that the rigour with which the data are used is misplaced in view of errors of response, collection and compilation. But there was never a suggestion that the government used its leverage to change figures in the direction which made it politically more expedient.

Several current indicators such as the consumer price index, the rate of unemployment, the merchandise trade balance, and the monthly gross domestic product have marked effects on the money and security markets, particularly when their release creates a surprise in the minds of market agents. Advance knowledge of the figures could entail very important commercial advantages should the holder of such knowledge decide to apply it to financial speculative purpose. Nothing would destroy more quickly the confidence in which business holds the statistical agency than if one such case took place and it were shown that the agency had either succumbed to political pressure or worse still had used its inside knowledge to further the fortunes of its officials. No such event has marked the history of Statistics Canada and that too is a contributing factor to the relative ease with which the agency can persuade business to provide it with information.

V. Concluding considerations

It does not follow from any of this that in order to run a successful statistical agency each and every one of these measures has to be duplicated. Firstly, they appear here as examples. Secondly, many of them are profoundly anchored in the Canadian institutional setting and lastly, they represent an expensive but long standing allocation of resources.

But it does follow that securing cooperation and attaining high rates of response are priorities that do not come free and therefore in making budgetary calculations they have to be explicitly factored in.

The management of Statistics Canada has gone on record as saying that it is inefficient statistically and financially to conceive of large samples in the design of sample surveys in the knowledge that the rate of response is going to be low and that, therefore, the greater the sample the greater the chances of ending up with a useable number of responses. Another strategic principle expected to govern the agency's survey-taking programme is to attempt to get things right the first time. Statistics Canada's expenses on editing may average as much as 50 per cent of its total expenses on survey processing. The challenge is to find out whether a one time investment in educating respondents and reaching agreements with them on how to interpret questions and how to reply in line with standard concepts is not significantly cheaper than an ongoing investment in editing routines and applications.

The same reasoning holds for imputation in two guises. Firstly, there is the imputation for missing records which implies the artificial expansion of samples to meet stated coefficient of variation targets and the continuing uncertainty about the robustness of the imputation assumptions. There are situations where non-respondents can be regarded as probability sub-samples of a master sample but such situations tend to be exceptional. Accordingly, an investment to persuade potential non-respondents to cooperate with the statistical agency and comply with its survey, can lead to considerable economies elsewhere.

A second application of this principle is to the current collection of data. Roughly ten per cent of the money that Statistics Canada spends on data collection conducted by local offices is assigned to follow-up activities. Some of these follow-up activities are inevitable. They have to do with the detection of businesses that have either ceased to exist or changed ownership or trade name, accountant, location or activity. Other follow-up activities are avoidable. They have to do with late filers, respondents who for one reason or another did not forward filled-in questionnaire or were not ready when contacted over the telephone. Since most current estimates are released at fixed dates and for their release to be possible a certain proportion of respondents must have filed their replies, last minutes follow-up is invariably a costly activity.

To keep it within more manageable proportions, Statistics Canada has invested in systems that allow it to come to firmer agreements with respondents and to continue experimenting with systems that will make it as easy as possible for respondents to file their replies. The existing systems – mostly computer assisted telephone interviewing – record an agreed day of the month, time of the day, name of contact and language of interview. The computer manages the timetables and reminds the interviewer that the scheduled time is up. The interviewer has the flexibility to add to the interview whatever elements of personal contact he believes to be appropriate. This latter feature is not of great importance in very large cities but is of some significance in smaller agglomerations. There is also experimentation with touch-tone telephones, a technique which enables the respondent to punch in his replies by using the keypad on his telephone at a preassigned time – which could be outside office hours.

But to work out these agreements and to give respondents options, a network of contacts and trust must exist and it is to this that the considerations spelled out in this paper apply.

Statistics Canada has drawn a number of conclusions for itself and is trying to implement them. These conclusions can be shared by others interested in adopting similar measures.

- Do not exhaust budgets planning surveys and have nothing left over for respondent contacts, explanations and generally speaking, respondent support.
- The necessary means to persuade respondents are cumulative but span a wide range of activities including posture vis-à-vis the rest of government, general behaviour and ways in which that behaviour is perceived by the general public.
- Start building up confidence on the part of respondents and make sure that such confidence includes a feeling that the statistical office produces information relevant to them and not only to the higher instance of government.
- Remember that whereas it is important to have a legal basis for all statistical activities and that sanctions be part of that legal base, success is predicated upon the cooperativeness of the private sector. Business cannot all be fined

nor imprisoned even though sanctions may be a deterrent. Relevance and thoughtfulness are usually greater contributors to high response rate.

There is nothing very profound about these conclusions. In fact they seem self-evident. And yet it took Statistics Canada many, many years before it were to formulate them explicitly and even today some of the bad legacies from times past distort survey results. While not all experiences are exportable, some are and it would be a pity if in their enthusiasm for building new statistical systems, statistical offices in economies in transition did not invest the necessary resources in the infrastructure that makes this system of relations work.

Problems of Price Statistics: the Experience of Poland

Leszek Zienkowski
Research Centre for Statistical and Economic Analysis, Poland

While price indices in Poland have been compiled according to internationally accepted standards, they suffer from two problems typical of centrally-planned economies – spurious quality improvements and periodic shortages. The author believes that price inflation has generally been underestimated and suggests how the bias can be measured. Polish experience in international price comparison is also discussed. The main problem here is the difficulty of finding goods and service of comparable qualities, particularly for comparisons with Western countries.

I. Domestic price indices

Present methodology

The purpose for which price indices are calculated seems to be to give information to the user of statistics on *(i)* price movements (price indices as such), and *(ii)* relative price levels (structure of prices). In addition, price indices are calculated for the purpose of deflation from current to real values of certain economic aggregates such as production, consumption, capital formation, etc.

In Poland, the methodological approach to the compilation of price indices of industrial products, agricultural products, transport and communication services and other market services, as well as to the calculation of the consumer price index, does not differ substantially from that in Western European countries. This statement is valid also for Hungary, but not for most other countries of Central and Eastern Europe.

With the exception of agricultural products, the calculation of producer price indices is based on the prices of representative products and services. Market producer prices (ex factory prices) of representative industrial products are reported by enterprises according to the list agreed with the Central Statistical Office (CSO). About 800 representative products are covered. Prices are only reported by state and cooperative enterprises, because the private sector in manufacturing industry was very small in the past and the value of production did not exceed a few per cent.

As far as transport and communication services are concerned, the calculations are based on official list prices. For other producer services, the prices of representative services are reported by enterprises.

The calculation of the price index of agricultural products (prices received by farmers) uses both state procurement prices and free market prices reported by special price reporters affiliated to the CSO. The two types of prices are averaged using the estimated quantities traded in the two markets.

The index of consumer prices is based on almost one thousand representative goods and services sold in "socialised" trade and in the agricultural free markets. In addition, the prices of selected non-agricultural products sold in private trade and in non-registered trade are also collected. All prices are collected on the spot (shops, markets) by special price reporters employed by the CSO and are the prices actually paid by consumers.

The value of industrial production (sales of goods and the value of services sold) is used to weight the producer price indices. The values of purchases, either from family budget surveys or those estimated in the national accounts, are used in the calculation of the consumer price index. Laspeyres and Paasche formulas are used.

As far as we know, the Hungarian and Polish approach differs from that of other Central and Eastern European countries where price indices are often based on list prices only. In addition, other countries exclude new products of higher quality with rising prices. They also exclude free market agricultural prices from their indices.

The price indices of construction are estimated by the CSO using several kinds of information – prices of inputs, wages, list prices of selected structures, etc. – and cannot be regarded as highly reliable. (The methods are now being changed.) It should also be noted that as far as price indices of industrial products and of exports and imports are concerned, the least reliable part relates to machinery. It is often rather difficult to find comparable products in each of the different periods for which the price index is to be calculated. As a result, the reliability of the price index of fixed capital formation, which is composed of the sub-indices for construction and for machinery, is relatively low. The price index of inventories, which is estimated at the CSO from a number of different sources, must also be considered as rather unreliable.

Problems: past and future

The main problems with which the CSO was – and to some extent is still – confronted are the existence of widespread shortages and the fact that several prices have been administratively established and do not clear markets. Unlike the situation in a market economy, the prices of commodities within supposedly homogeneous commodity groups often moved in different ways. Thus it was extremely difficult to find a representative commodity whose price movement would be typical for the commodity group as a whole. This is a potential source of error which may have seriously affected the reliability of the final price index.

Another difficulty typical of a "shortage economy" is that products chosen as representative may be on sale in one month, disappear in the next month and be back on sale a month later.

Another problem is that, in the past, it often happened that the difference in the quality of a commodity entering the market was less than proportional to the difference in price in relation to other commodities of lower quality. Nevertheless, due to the permanent shortages and to the excess of demand over supply, consumers were ready to buy these commodities instead of the commodities which they would have preferred but which were not in sufficient supply. (This is often termed the "spill-over effects" of demand.) Since the price index was calculated using selected "representative commodities" which were supposed to be comparable in quality – at least in principle – in both the current and the base periods, the situation described above was responsible for underestimation of the true price increase, i.e. the price increase as measured after taking account of changes in quality. This problem affects indices of both producer and consumer prices.

Turning to the future, the Polish CSO, and probably statistical offices in other Central and Eastern European countries, are likely to face new difficulties of both a methodological and a practical nature. Methodological problems that will have to be resolved include the calculation of monthly price indices which will have to be adjusted for seasonality. The main new practical problem is how to obtain information on ex factory prices from the new, private-sector, enterprises.

Size of errors

It is very difficult to evaluate the amount by which price rises in Poland were underestimated. One possible approach consists of comparing price indices calculated for internal purposes with those which are calculated for international comparisons between Poland and Austria, carried out within the United Nations International Comparison Project (ICP).

Another possibility is to compare the real growth rates of industrial production calculated as deflated current values (with the use of the price index) with real growth rates calculated from physical quantities of representative products (weighted or unweighted). The difference may indicate whether one can expect large underestimation of price movements. This approach can be criticised on the grounds that the latter index can, as a rule, be expected to show a lower growth rate than that given by price deflation using a correctly calculated index. In Poland the difference between two such indices of industrial production amounted in the past to between 1½ and 2 percentage points at a time when the official growth rates, in real terms, were estimated at about 6 per cent.

In Poland, the differences between Laspeyres and Paasche price indices were relatively small and sometimes the latter has grown faster than the former. This indicates that Polish consumers could not adapt their consumption patterns to changing price and were forced to buy those commodities whose prices were rising faster than the average.

What has been written above indicates clearly that Polish price statistics have recorded the prices that were actually paid, but since they were not equilibrium prices their relative levels are distorted.

A final remark relates to the use of price indices for deflation purposes. It should be noted that price statistics were limited to market prices, as opposed to factor value prices, and that those market prices were used for deflating production which was valued at the prices actually received by enterprises. Thus one can question the validity of the calculations of real growth rates since these calculations were based on an economically meaningless system of prices. It seems to the author that this is a much larger problem than the problem of price statistics, but it will not be discussed here.

II. Price indices in the context of international comparisons

Poland and Hungary have taken part in the ICP from its beginning as well as in the comparisons within the Central and Eastern European countries organised by the CMEA. These studies have involved price and volume comparisons of consumption, capital formation and GDP.

The ICP methodology is well known and there is no need to repeat it here. Poland and some other CMEA countries carry out binary comparisons with Austria, which acts as a "bridge country" between the CMEA countries and the other countries which participate in ICP. One could point to certain differences between comparisons within OECD countries and those in which Austria acts as the "bridge country". In the former, the Geary-Khamis method was used for aggregation while in the latter group the Fisher method was used. In the author's opinion, however, the most important point, in practice, is not the formula but the problem of quality differences. It was very difficult in the Polish/Austria comparisons to find representative products which are both similar in quality and typical of consumption and capital formation in both countries. According to the point of view prevailing in Poland, it is better to introduce certain adjustment coefficients than to compare prices of products which differ in quality. "Differences in quality" means not only physical differences (such as different percentage of fat in milk, different quality of wool or cotton, differences in petrol consumption by passenger cars or trucks, etc.) but also differences in fashion or in those characteristics which make a product more or less attractive to the buyer. In the Poland/Austria comparisons we tried to eliminate at least the former types of quality differences. We were aware that this involved value judgements since we were using the opinions of commodity experts from different branches, and not using the hedonic methods to evaluate the impact on prices of the differences in quality. In our opinion, however, the potential misjudgement of experts is less dangerous than basing comparisons on prices of commodities which are not comparable in quality. The final error is smaller in the former case. In our opinion, the Polish experts were inclined to overvalue the quality of Polish products so that the final price index underestimates the differences in price levels. As a result, the real level of GDP per capita was overestimated.

The methodology of international comparisons within the CMEA countries is very similar to that used in ICP and there is no need to describe it in detail. The Soviet Union performs a role similar to that of Austria. There are binary comparisons between each country and the Soviet Union which is the "star" in the whole system of comparisons. The Fisher formula is used for comparisons with the Soviet Union.

According to the author's opinion, the results of those comparisons are less reliable than the ICP results for the following reasons:

i) Price statistics in a number of CMEA countries are not well developed. In particular, list prices are used instead of actual market prices;

ii) Compared with the ICP, less attention is paid to the description of representative products and to their quality differences. (Quality differences may generally be smaller within the CMEA group than in the case of Poland/Austria comparisons, but they still exist between Soviet Union, Poland and other countries.) As a result, non-comparable products may have been taken as representative products for the CMEA comparisons.

Nevertheless the results are by no means meaningless. In the author's opinion, they show the differences between countries as far as general price levels and real volumes are concerned.

It may be of interest to note that the difference in GDP per capita between Hungary and Poland according to ICP was 127 (Poland = 100) in 1985 and the same difference according to internal comparisons within CMEA countries was estimated for the same year as equal to 122 (Poland = 100).

The System of National Accounts in the Countries in Transition

Laszlo Drechsler
Central Statistical Office, Hungary

This paper provides an overview of the problems that will be faced by Central and Eastern European countries in moving from the Material Product System (MPS) to the OECD-UN System of National Accounts. Apart from the treatment of services, the two systems also differ in their treatment of depreciation and losses, and the MPS is relatively underdeveloped with regard to financial transactions.

I. Introduction

The profound economic, social and political changes which are taking place in Central and Eastern Europe have also brought important changes in respect of the statistics required in these countries. All statistical offices in these countries (hereafter: countries in transition) have launched major programmes for the transformation of their statistical systems in order to meet the needs of the changing economy and society. In these developments the extension and promotion of national accounting systems play a central role. One of the most important characteristics of these changes is the increased interest in using more intensively the United Nations System of National Accounts (SNA).

There are many common features in the countries in transition in respect of their national accounting developments. All these countries applied exclusively or primarily the Material Product System (MPS) for their national accounting purposes. The MPS was worked out and approved by the Council for Mutual Economic Assistance (CMEA). All countries in transition have some knowledge about the SNA (or, at least, about the differences between the MPS and the SNA) thanks to the work of the group on SNA/MPS links, sponsored by the United Nations since the beginning of the sixties. There are also many similarities in the social and economic developments of these countries: a substantial shift from the state and cooperative sectors to the private sector; a considerable increase in the share of small units in the economy; the strengthening of the role of the market in economic relations and; the decreasing (or disappearing) importance of central planning, at least in its traditional function.

There are also differences among the countries in transition. Some of them have already accumulated substantial experiences in SNA type calculations. Hungary, for instance, has compiled and published regularly, since the end of the sixties, SNA type production account and income and outlay account figures. Poland has also compiled similar figures, although for a shorter period. Other countries also have some experience, at least in Gross Domestic Product calculations; however, this was done in most cases on an experimental basis or for international comparison purposes only.

Although all countries in transition seem to be moving in the same direction, there are important differences in the stage of economic and social transformation reached by these countries in the middle of 1990, and this inevitably has an impact on the developments in their national accounting. Some of the countries have already made important steps towards the use of the SNA in their national statistics; others are only planning to do so. At the time of writing this paper it is not entirely clear how far the final objectives of the development of national accounting, as planned by the different countries, are close to each other. Some of the countries may opt to use exclusively the SNA as their national accounting system and to drop the MPS. Others may prefer to use both systems, at least for a certain time. Again others may opt for continuing to use the MPS as the main national accounting system, supplemented by various SNA elements, like Gross Domestic Product calculations.

Whatever the option of particular countries in transition, there are a number of common problems to be solved. The purpose of this paper is to provide assistance to these countries by listing the tasks involved in transforming the national accounting system and by giving advice on how to carry them out. Primarily it aims to help those countries which would like to introduce the SNA to as full an extent as possible. The present paper is restricted to the conceptual problems of national accounting. Organizational problems, such as how to get the basic data under the new conditions (registers, sample surveys etc.), will not be dealt with here.

II. Production accounts

General considerations

Production account statistics, i.e. statistics on gross output, intermediate consumption, final consumption, capital formation, exports and imports, is the field in which most progress was achieved by the work on SNA/MPS links. Until the 25th session of the UN Statistical Commission (February 1989) this work was restricted to identifying the differences between the MPS and corresponding SNA concepts, and to describing what adjustments should be made (what items should be added/deducted) in order to get a particular aggregate of one system from the related aggregates in the other without, however, bringing the two systems closer to each other.

The 1989 meeting of the Statistical Commission constituted a turning point in the work on the SNA/MPS links. All countries from centrally-planned economies present at this session expressed interest in bringing the two systems closer to each other and offered a number of concessions on the MPS side to achieve this goal. At various meetings of the CMEA countries later in 1989 this intention was confirmed and elaborated, and at a joint meeting of SNA and MPS experts in December 1989 in Moscow, a programme was agreed on the integration of the two systems. Pursuing this programme, the CMEA Secretariat started to revise the MPS with the main objective of bringing it into line with the SNA, and the authors of the new SNA were requested to insert into the draft text a number of additions or modifications taking care of the special conditions and circumstances of the countries with centrally-planned economies.

While many of the elements of the 1989 December programme are very useful in the present circumstances, the logic of this programme may be questioned in view of the developments which have taken place since then. The countries in Central and Eastern Europe are losing their centrally-planned character and becoming market economies. Most likely, it is no longer the case that they would like to modify their MPS statistics (by bringing them closer to the SNA), but they would like to use the SNA as such, with or without a modified MPS. This is why this note tries to present the essential tasks in national accounting as the introduction of the SNA rather than as the modification of the MPS. It is hoped, however, that the content of this paper may provide services also to those countries which would like to remain on the December 1989 programme and continue with a modified MPS.

As it emerged from the 1989 discussions, the differences between the SNA and the MPS as regards production account statistics can be grouped into three broad categories.

a) Differences stemming from different economic theories (e.g. the different treatment of "non-material" services);

b) Differences stemming from different institutional arrangements (e.g. most banks in centrally-planned economies are not profit oriented and behave like public administration units);

c) Incidental differences stemming from the fact that the two systems were drawn up independently from each other and, in a number of cases, different conventions were adopted (e.g. business travel expenses are treated as intermediate consumption in the SNA, but as final consumption in the MPS).

As to the differences mentioned in the first group, they lose their importance as soon as a country decides to compile SNA type aggregates. With this decision the country implicitly accepts that it is willing to accept the underlying economic theory of the SNA (either exclusively, or jointly, with the underlying economic theory of the MPS).

As to the differences mentioned in the second group, they are also losing their importance with the substantial economic and social changes taking place in the countries in transition. Nevertheless, they cannot be neglected entirely, since a number of special features, such as the heavy subsidisation of housing, may continue for a long time. This is why the request made in December 1989 to supplement the SNA with specific rules and explanations to help the adaptation of the system to special circumstances is still justified.

As to the incidental differences, their removal has already been agreed upon in the 1989 December meeting. Whether their removal takes place for a particular country by aligning the MPS with the SNA, or by discontinuing with the MPS altogether, depends on the decision taken by each country as to whether it wants to use both systems in the future, or only the SNA. In any case, great attention to these incidental differences should be paid in the transition period, since they play an important role in the introduction of the SNA methodology. A detailed inventory of the incidental differences in the concepts of the production account statistics was given in a document prepared for the 1989 December meeting (UNSO, 1989). It is not intended to reproduce in the present paper all these differences; however, the most important of them will be referred to in describing the tasks that countries in transition will need to to accomplish in the field of national accounting.

Treatment of non material services

The most characteristic and important difference between the two systems is in the treatment of "non-material" services – personal and social services such as beauticians, cinemas, launderies and sporting events, financial and certain business services and all government services. The SNA treats these services as being inside the production boundary, while in the MPS they are treated as redistribution flows, i.e. as being outside the production boundary.

It should be emphasized that the difference is much more in the treatment than in the availability of statistics. There are several tables in the MPS containing information on non-material services. Thus the task of the countries which are starting to compile SNA production aggregates is not so much the collection of additional data but more the rearrangement of the data on non-material services which are already available in the system. This rearrangement involves two specific tasks: *(a)* to separate non-material service flows from other redistribution flows such as interest payments and *(b)* to change the treatment of non-material services, i.e. to bring them inside the production boundary.

Statistical units for production statistics

In the SNA, the observation unit to be used for production statistics is the establishment, i.e. that part of the enterprise which is, as far as possible, homogeneous from the point of view of the activity carried out and located in a single place. The MPS does not use the term establishment; the observation unit proposed is the enterprise, or, for some purposes, a homogeneous unit within the enterprise, referred to as an "accounting unit". While the accounting unit has some similarities with the SNA establishment its content is to some extent different. For example, in general, only those activities are separated from the rest of the enterprise which belong to another main branch of activity.

In the MPS, the income and capital finance statistics are far less developed than in the SNA. This is presumably the main reason why the MPS can get along with only one kind of observation unit throughout the whole system, whereas in the SNA, separate kinds of observation units are needed for production statistics (establishments or similar units) and for financial statistics (enterprises or similar institutional units). Perhaps it is not wrong to say that MPS tries to use an intermediate type of unit which may serve the purposes of both production and financial statistics. It is very likely, however, that with the development of the financial sector, the countries in transition will not be able to avoid accepting a dichotomy in statistical units as proposed in the SNA.

As regards production statistics, the main task for the countries in transition seems to be to introduce establishment type units into their national accounting systems. In this respect the recommendations of the International Standard Industrial Classification (ISIC) Rev.3, or those of the draft new SNA should be followed.

Attention should be paid in this connection also to the proposed treatment of ancillary activities. In the SNA, ancillary activities are distinguished from secondary activities. While the latter include those activities which, for practical reasons, cannot be separated from the establishment's main activities (and so need to be treated as produced within the same establishment), ancillary activities are those intra-enterprise activities (e.g. repair of own equipment, transportation of purchased or own produced goods) for which no separation is recommended even if it were possible in practice. This type of distinction is not entirely unknown in the MPS; however, it is much less elaborated than that which is proposed in the ISIC or SNA.

Gross output, intermediate consumption, value added

There are a number of differences in the gross output, intermediate consumption and value added concepts between the SNA and MPS, in addition to those already mentioned. Most of these additional differences belong to the "incidental differences" category and are described in detail in the paper which was prepared for the 1989 December meeting (UNSO, 1989). As already noted, this meeting accepted a programme to remove the incidental differences (or at least most of them), and since then a preliminary draft version of various chapters of the "integrated MPS" was prepared by the CMEA Secretariat in which most of the incidental differences have already been eliminated. For instance, in this new "integrated MPS" business travel expenses are treated as intermediate consumption (as in the SNA) and not as final consumption. Nevertheless, for the countries in transition, in which the traditional MPS rules have been applied till now, the removal of the incidental differences is still a task ahead of them.

Some of the differences affect gross output and intermediate consumption in a parallel way without affecting value added. For instance, gross output of restaurants, cafes and other catering units equals the value of the sales by these units in the SNA, but is defined as the value of trade margin (sales minus purchases of raw materials) in the MPS. However, since the purchases of raw materials by the catering units are treated as intermediate consumption in the SNA, but not in the MPS, the value added of the catering units is the same in the two systems. The elimination of these type of differences has somewhat lower priority, since both for national analytical uses and international comparisons, value added has primary importance and not gross output and intermediate consumption.

There also are some differences in the valuation of production. Both systems use production aggregates expressed at market prices and at prices excluding some taxes and including some subsidies. Market prices are almost the same in the two systems and the differences (e.g. the inclusion of tips in the SNA but their exclusion in the MPS) are relatively small. More differences can be observed in respect of the valuation excluding taxes, in spite of the fact that this type of valuation has practically the same function in the two systems. The differences stem from the fact that the scope of the taxes (subsidies) excluded (included) is different in the two systems. It should be noted that in a number of countries in transition taxation systems are changing and getting closer to those of market economies. This may bring their valuation methods closer to those of the SNA.

There are a number of other valuation differences between the two systems, described in the document referred to earlier (UNSO, 1989). They mostly relate to items for which imputed prices are used (e.g. consumption from own production, wages and salaries in kind, own account capital formation). Special mention should be made of the valuation differences of goods and services which are highly subsidized (housing rents, medicines, etc.). This is one of the fields where the SNA is planning to change its valuation methods in order to meet the requirement of the countries where highly subsidized items have a relatively high importance.

Consumption of fixed capital

Consumption of fixed capital has a somewhat different role in the production statistics of the two systems. While in the MPS, net concepts (i.e. after the deduction of consumption of fixed capital) are mostly used, in the SNA gross concepts, (i.e. before the deduction of consumption of fixed capital) have the central role. Views may be divided as to whether or not this is a conceptual difference between the two systems. In the view of the author, the reason for giving priority to the gross concepts in the SNA is the consideration that data on consumption of fixed capital are, in general, not sufficiently reliable. It is considered, therefore, as being more appropriate not to burden the production concepts, which have to play a central role in the system, with the inaccuracies of the consumption of fixed capital aggregate. If consumption of fixed capital figures were sufficiently reliable, net product concepts would probably play a larger role in the production statistics of the SNA than gross concepts.

In the MPS, it seems that, similar considerations did not play any role in drawing up the production statistics of the system. Consequently, for a country in transition, when transforming its national accounting system, the main question to be answered in this respect is the following: are the data on consumption of fixed capital sufficiently reliable or not? If the answer is yes, preference could be given to net product concepts for domestic analytic uses, although it should be noted that *gross* concepts also are needed for international comparison purposes. If the answer is no, preference should be given to gross concepts even for domestic analytical uses, as recommended in the SNA. Attention should be drawn in this respect to the possibility that the economic and social changes taking place in the countries in transition (e.g. the increasing share of the private sector) may adversely influence the accuracy of the data on consumption of fixed capital.

The valuation of consumption of fixed capital is also different in the two systems. In the SNA, consumption of fixed capital is valued at current replacement cost. In the MPS no year to year revaluations are proposed for fixed assets and consumption of fixed capital is calculated on the basis of book values, which may be modified by occasional general revaluations of fixed assets. The MPS method may have worked sufficiently well in periods when no, or very low, inflation affected these countries; however, at present, inflation rates are relatively high in practically all countries in transition. This is also a reason for trying to introduce the SNA type calculations in these countries in respect of consumption of fixed capital.

Final consumption

There is a consumption concept which, in principle, should be the same in the two systems. This concept was referred to in both systems as "total consumption of the population" (TCP); however, the new draft SNA changed the terminology and refers to it as "actual consumption of households". TCP was worked out in the early sixties by experts working on the SNA/MPS links. It has already been introduced into the 1968 version of the MPS, and it was introduced into the SNA by a document published in the seventies complementing the 1968 version of the SNA.

However, it turns out from a recent study by the Conference of European Statisticians, (CES, 1989), that in spite of a common early history, TCP followed a different path in the SNA and in the MPS. This was because there was no organ to coordinate the development of the concept. Consequently, there are a number of differences between TCP as defined in the MPS and as defined in the SNA. Most of these differences have an incidental character, without having any rationale in economic theory. The 1989 December meeting agreed to eliminate most, of these differences, almost exclusively by aligning the MPS measure with the SNA one. It is very likely that the "integrated MPS" that is being prepared by the CMEA Secretariat will achieve this objective. However, for a country in transition, which until now applied a traditional MPS, a number of changes will have to be made in measuring consumption.

MPS has no concept corresponding to the SNA's Household Consumption Expenditure (HCE). HCE covers that part of the TCP which is financed by the households themselves. If a country in transition decides to apply the SNA in its full extent, the explicit presentation of the HCE is also needed. This does not constitute a difficult task, since this concept differs from the TCP only by the simple deletion of that part of the consumption which is financed by sectors other than households.

More difficult for the countries in transition is to introduce into their national accounting practice Government Consumption Expenditure and Government Final Consumption. The earlier work on SNA/MPS links covered the government consumption concepts only in a superficial way and did not identify the differences between the two systems. Comparability between the two systems was limited not only by incidental differences, but also by differences in institutional arrangements.

The "Government" as defined in the SNA has no exact equivalent in the MPS. "Institutions and organizations catering to collective community needs" of the MPS is the closest counterpart to the SNA "Government", but there are a number of differences between the two. For instance, the MPS concept covers a number of organisations which are treated in the SNA as private non profit institutions (e.g. trade unions and political parties), and also some units which, in the SNA, belong to the enterprise sector (e.g. insurance companies). Some transactions are also treated differently, e.g. expenditure on military durables is treated as consumption in the SNA, but, at least partially, as capital formation in the MPS.

Consequently, for Government Consumption, the countries in transition cannot make as much use of the already available knowledge as is the case for other aggregates of the production account. The introduction of the SNA concepts in this field should be based on the text of the draft new SNA. The institutional changes going on in the countries in transition may also facilitate the introduction of the SNA concepts.

Capital formation

As earlier work on the SNA/MPS links has shown, the capital formation concepts in the two systems are very close to each other. The differences are few in number and they are relatively small. Some of the differences related to total capital formation, others only to the borderline between the two main components – fixed capital formation and increase in stocks. All these differences are described in detail in the document prepared for the 1989 December meeting (UNSO, 1989).

There are several changes planned in the new SNA with respect to the scope of capital formation. At the time of writing this paper, it is not yet known what the final decision will be, but it is very likely that the scope of capital formation will be extended to include the costs of mineral exploration, the value of software, some intellectual property flows and, perhaps, the cost of research and development. All these items are excluded from capital formation as defined in the MPS. If these changes are accepted this will require modifications not only in countries in transition but also in traditional market economy countries, since in most of them these items were treated as current production costs and therefore outside the scope of capital formation.

Exports and imports

SNA and MPS external trade flows differ not only because of the differences in the production boundary (non-material services are excluded from MPS exports and imports), but also because the boundaries of the domestic economy are differently defined. SNA has an explicit definition of "resident units" based on whether the unit's centre of economic interest is inside or outside the territory of the given country. In the MPS there is no explicit definition of resident units and as to the implicit definition of resident units that can be derived from the rules related to particular flows, it differs in many respects from the SNA definition. Thus, the countries in transition will not only have to modify the content of exports and imports flows, but will also have to correct the boundaries of the national economy.

Losses

There are substantial differences between the two systems with respect to the treatment of losses. These differences affect the comparability between the SNA and MPS in respect of several of the main aggregates of the production account – intermediate consumption, consumption of fixed capital, capital formation and value added. Details about these differences are given in the 1989 December document referred to earlier.

It seems that the main reason for these differences stems from the fact that, in the MPS, there is nothing which corresponds to the "revaluation account" of the SNA (more precisely to one of its components which is referred to in the draft new

SNA as "Other Changes in the Volume of Assets Account"). Because the MPS has no revaluation account, consistency between the transaction tables and the balance sheets can only be obtained by charging all losses, including so called capital losses (e.g. consequences of natural catastrophes) against some transaction aggregate.

It should be noted that the countries in transition, even in the past, followed the MPS rules in respect of the treatment of the losses only with a number of deviations. This may facilitate the transition to the SNA rules, since many of the deviations brought the national systems closer to the solutions adopted in market economies.

III. Financial accounts

General problems

The term "financial accounts" is used in this document as a generic term for the income and outlay, capital finance and revaluation accounts as well as for the balance sheets. The task of establishing SNA type financial statistics will be much more difficult for countries in transition than is the case for production account statistics. This is mainly because in the MPS there is no real counterpart to the SNA financial accounts, and countries do not have sufficient experiences in this type of compilation. For the same reasons the progress achieved by the work of the group on SNA/MPS links in respect of financial statistics is also very limited.

Institutional sectors

As already mentioned earlier, in the MPS there are no equivalents to the institutional sectors of the SNA. The MPS distinguishes only "ownership sectors" (state, cooperative and private sectors, with some further subdivisions), which, however, differ in many respects from the SNA sectors. There is no distinction in the MPS between enterprises and the rest of the economy; there is no separation between the financial and non-financial sectors; "population" in the MPS is not the same as "households" in the SNA; and there is no equivalent in the MPS to the private non-profit institutions sector of the SNA. These differences between the national accounting systems were partly explained by the differences in the institutional arrangements between the two groups of countries; thus, many of them were not only simple incidental differences as are most of the differences in production statistics. In centrally-planned countries, where the overwhelming part of the economy was owned or controlled by the government, financial aspects of transactions were less relevant than in market economies.

With the substantial economic and social changes which are taking place in the countries in transition, the financial aspects are becoming much more important. The need for SNA type financial statistics successively strengthens in all countries in transition, and sooner or later it will become essential to start using the same types of institutional units and institutional sectors as recommended by the SNA.

One of the most important changes required in the transformation of the statistics of the countries in transition is to accept the SNA dichotomy of transactors – i.e.

establishment type units for production statistics and enterprise type units for financial statistics – and to introduce the concept of institutional units as recommended in the SNA. An institutional unit is defined in the SNA as an economic entity which is capable, in its own right, of owning assets, incurring liabilities and engaging in economic activities and transactions with other entities. It follows from this definition that it must be possible to compile a full set of accounts and to draw up a balance sheet for an institutional unit.

The next step is to partition the economy into a number of (institutional) sectors and sub-sectors, as recommended in the SNA. The sectors and sub-sectors consist of groups of resident institutional units. The four main sectors of the economy are:

The non-financial corporate sector
The financial corporate sector
The general government sector
The household sector

Though this breakdown is substantially different from the sectoral breakdown applied in traditional MPS statistics, its introduction does not raise any special difficulties in practice.

Income and outlay

Although various income concepts are defined in the text of the MPS and are used by the countries in transition, these concepts, and their constituant elements, are substantially different from the income concepts recommended in the SNA. There are two major problems with the income concepts of the MPS: *(a)* it is very difficult to create analytically useful concepts if income generated in the non material sphere (e.g. the salary of a hospital doctor) is treated differently from income generated in the material sphere (e.g. the salary of a factory employee), and *(b)* there is no clear distinction between different types of transactions in the system; in particular, payments which have a redistributive character (e.g. taxes or gifts) are often combined under the same heading as transactions in financial assets and liabilities (e.g. loans or repayment of loans). While the former group of transactions affects the *size* of the wealth of the transactors involved, the latter affects only the *composition* of wealth.

As a consequence, in the MPS no aggregates can be compiled such as disposable income or saving, which are among the most important analytical concepts of the SNA. Perhaps it is not an exaggeration to say that the absence of these concepts from the MPS constitutes the most serious weakness of the system. How much the wealth of a given institutional sector, or of the whole nation, changes as a result of production, consumption and redistributive transactions is important information no matter how the economy is organised.

There are a number of additional tasks for the countries in transition in establishing their income and outlay statistics. Only the two most important ones will be mentioned here:

- Primary incomes (compensation of employees, income from property, indirect taxes net of subsidies) received from, or paid to the rest of the world should be distinguished from other transactions with the rest of the world. This is needed to make it possible to calculate Gross National Product.

- Current transfers should be separated from capital transfers. The former are made out of the income of the current period, while the latter are made out of wealth. This distinction is needed because current transfers affect disposable income and saving while capital transfers do not.

Capital finance statistics

What are referred to in the SNA as capital finance statistics, are almost entirely missing from the MPS and from the national accounting practices of the countries in transition. To some extent this is understandable, since in the conditions of a centrally-planned economy the need for such statistics was limited. For instance, in a country where banks are not generally profit-oriented and where there are no shares or other securities, there is no need to have a detailed classification of financial assets and liabilities.

The task of establishing SNA type capital finance statistics in a country in transition is complex. New concepts have to be introduced or distinguished from already existing concepts and new classifications have to be worked out, not to mention the difficult organisational problems to be solved in order to obtain the basic data needed. In view of the growing share of the private sector and the growing role of the banks and other financial institutions in the economy, a relatively high priority should be attached to developing capital finance statistics in spite of the difficulties involved.

Revaluation statistics

In the SNA, the revaluation accounts constitute the bridge between the production, income-outlay and capital finance accounts on one hand, and the balance sheets on the other. Changes in the value of assets and liabilities (and, consequently, in net worth) reflected in the balance sheets may take place not only as results of production, consumption, and redistribution but also for other reasons, like natural calamities, general price level changes, and changes in relative prices. These latter changes in values are reflected in the revaluation accounts. In the MPS and, presumably, in the practice of the countries in transition there is no counterpart to the revaluation accounts.

It should be noted that though revaluation accounts have a clear function in the SNA, owing to the practical difficulties involved in compiling them a number of countries with market economy do not yet construct them, and want to introduce them only at a later stage. The same type of practical difficulties may also be encountered by the countries in transition; thus, it is perhaps fair to say that somewhat lower priority should be attached to the introduction of revaluation accounts than to the development of other parts of the SNA.

Balance sheets

It is very likely that most countries in transition have already experience in compiling balance sheets. Nevertheless, there are a number of differences between the balance sheets of the two systems. Most of them relate to financial assets and liabilities, but there are also some differences in the items covered by the balance sheets and in the valuation of various assets. It seems that relatively high priority, in both the SNA and the MPS, is given to only one part of the balance sheets – stocks of fixed capital.

IV. Accounts versus tables

SNA is a set of accounts while MPS is a set of "sources and uses" tables, referred to in the original language as "balances". This is not merely a difference in form. Accounts are disciplined by the double entry bookkeeping rules – the same transaction has to be recorded on the debit side of one account and on the credit side of another account. On the other hand, sources and uses tables, which formally may look exactly like accounts, enjoy a larger liberty: they can be compiled, at least in principle, independently from each other.

The greater flexibility of the sources and uses tables no doubt has some advantages. In this way it is possible to adapt the measurement method to the purpose it is intended to serve. For example, consumption from own production can be valued at producers prices in production statistics, but at consumer prices in measuring consumption or levels of living. For most users, however, this type of "flexibility" causes more problems than benefits. The consistency between the various parts of the system will suffer, and a number of contradictions may arise. It is suggested, therefore, that in transforming the national accounts to the SNA, not only the content should be modified, but also the form.

It should be noted that the account form, though much more disciplined than the source and use table form, does not by any means eliminate all flexibility. From this point of view, the new SNA will substantially differ from the present version. The draft text proposes that in addition to the core accounts, which are subject to very strict consistency rules, "satellite accounts", may also be compiled. For these accounts, the concepts, definitions and classifications may deviate to some extent from those in the basic part of the system. Furthermore, it is planned to have a separate chapter of the system which deals with the problems of the application of the integrated framework of the SNA to specific circumstances and needs.

References

1. Conference of European Statisticians, Geneva (1989) *Total Consumption of the Population in the System of National Accounts and in the System of Statistical Balances of the National Economy* (CES/WP22/103).
2. United Nations Statistical Office, New York (1989) *Differences in Concepts and Definitions Between the System of National Accounts and the Balance of the National Economy.*

Input-Output Statistics: Their Role in Statistical Programmes

Norbert Rainer
Central Statistical Office, Austria

This paper describes the input-output statistics presently available in the Central and Eastern European countries and compares them with input-output tables compiled in countries using the System of National Accounts (SNA). The author argues that input-output tables have two important roles – as a means of improving the reliability and consistency of the national accounts and for their uses in economic analysis. Input-output tables have been used for studies of energy use, industrial pollution, price inflation and trade and industrial policy. These are all important policy concerns in the countries of Central and Eastern Europe.

I. Introduction

This document tries to present some reflections on the role that input-output statistics should have within a system of economic statistics, especially within a system of national accounts. Special attention is given to the situation in industrialised market economies like member states of the OECD. The aspects treated here do not refer to the status of one single country nor are they based on special reviews undertaken in OECD countries. They rather reflect personal experience of the author as a staff member of the Austrian Central Statistical Office. What seems to be most important is the fact that the role of input-output statistics is predominantly derived from a system's point of view viz. the System of National Accounts (SNA). The overall guideline in the discussion of the role of input-output statistics is therefore the position of input-output statistics within the national accounts system. National accounts concepts are here seen on the basis of the 1968 SNA, which is now undergoing a review that will change many concepts and definitions in detail, but will not change the basic structure of the accounting framework. This especially applies to the input-output part of the system.

This document gives a short listing of typical applications of input-output in economic analysis and policy advice in industrialised market economies. This inventory will be an incomplete one. Here special emphasis will be given to analytic and policy questions especially related to problems when moving from centrally-planned to market economies. The changes in the respective economies will be such that they must be regarded as changes in the structure of the economy. Therefore, a data base of a structural character will be of great importance.

After a short evaluation of the role of input-output in the central and eastern European countries (CEECs) in Section II, Sections III and IV examine the role of input-output in the market economies on the basis of SNA concepts. A distinction will be made between input-output as a statistical system (Section III) and input-output as an analytical instrument (Section IV). Within the role of input-output as a statistical system (make-use matrices) three aspects are pointed out:

- Input-output as a core of the accounts of the national accounts system;
- Input-output as a conceptual and accounting framework supporting the transition from MPS to SNA;
- Input-output as a guideline for developing and improving basic statistics.

II. Input-output statistics in the Central and Eastern European Countries

In the CEECs, input-output tables are conceptually based on the System of Balances of the National Economy. Within this system the "material balance" – which shows sources and use of material products and services related to the material production – is the conceptual and also the numerical starting point for elaborating input-output tables. To this end, the institutional branches of the material balance are further disaggregated, the inputs are attributed to the activities performed and a uniform valuation of the flows of material products is introduced. Thus, input-output tables are to be viewed as an integral part of the System of Balances: the theoretical and methodological principles adopted in the construction of the System of Balances also apply to input-output tables; there are identical definitions between the System of Balances and input-output tables; and the basic figures calculated for the material balance are the starting points in the preparation of input-output tables. The conceptual frame of input-output tables within the System of Balances corresponds to the open Leontief model with the well-known three quadrants (quadrant I: inter-industry flows; quadrant II: utilisation of final product; quadrant III: structure of national income).

Compiling input-output tables has been a regular task of the statistical offices in the CEECs. The tables are compiled usually within a relatively short span of time; they are also relatively detailed as regards the number of branches distinguished. In most of the CEECs the level of disaggregation is between 60 and 100 branches, in some countries the level of disaggregation is much higher, at least for benchmark years. There seem to exist in the CEECs the same kind of problems of inconsistency and incompleteness of the basic data as in other countries so that balancing is also a difficult and important phase in the compilation process. Furthermore, there are usually discrepancies in the aggregated numerical results between the input-output tables and the material balance. These discrepancies are due to the fact that input-ouput works on a more detailed level than national accounts (material balance), and that input-output is forced to achieve consistency between supply and use at a very detailed level.

There is also great experience in the CEECs regarding application of input-output for analytical purposes. What is to be mentioned first is the role of input-output in elaborating the national economic plans. The input-output tables compiled by the statistical offices are of course not the only instruments in that field and there are in addition special input-output table, more detailed and in physical terms. Nevertheless, input-output tables have been constructed with a view to their use as a planning instrument. In addition, we can find many other kinds of analytical use of input-output in the CEECs. These range from traditional multiplier analysis to macro-economic modelling and forecasting, from linkage analysis to optimisation models, and from comparative analysis to sectorial studies and studies of labour inputs.

Summing up, input-output – both as a statistical system and as an analytical instrument – has a prominent place in economic statistics and economic analysis in the CEECs. One of the most important roles of input-output in the past (viz. input-output for planning purposes) will of course cease or has already ceased in the ongoing transition from centrally-planned to market economies.

III. Input-output as a statistical system

Input-output within the System of National Accounts (SNA 1968)

In the System of National Accounts (SNA 1968) input-output is an integrated part of the overall system of national accounts. Comparing the situation of input-output within the System of Material Balances with that in the SNA context one might consider input-output to be integrated not only as regards the definition and concepts of the transactors but also as regards the accounting structure.

The SNA distinguishes between accounts for production, consumption expenditure and capital formation (level I-accounts) and accounts for income and outlay and capital finance (level II-accounts). This dual approach is one of the basic characteristics of the SNA. To the duality of accounts corresponds the duality of classes of transactors based on different statistical units: producing units are the base for the level I-accounts and institutional units for the level II-accounts. For the depiction of the production process the appropriate statistical unit is the establishment, which is a homogeneous production unit; for the income and finance operations the appropriate statistical unit is the enterprise, which has autonomy in financial matters.

Input-output in the SNA is situated within the level I-accounts, of which the production and commodity accounts are the basis for input-output tables. Production accounts show production revenues (gross output) and production costs, the latter being subdivided into intermediate consumption and, as a balancing item, value added. Out of value added compensation of employees, consumption of fixed capital and net indirect taxes have to be financed, the rest of value added being operating surplus.

In the commodity accounts, supply (domestic production and imports) and use (intermediate and final use) of the goods and services are balanced. Using a corresponding classification of activities and commodities yields a system of cross-classified accounts: production accounts established according to a kind of activity classification (industries) show output and intermediate consumption by commodities; commodity accounts established according to a similar kind of commodity classification show domestic supply and intermediate consumption by industries.

The system of production and commodity accounts can also be looked at using a matrix presentation. In a matrix presentation these accounts are then referred to as the make-use (absorption) system. Four matrices have to be distinguished:

- The make matrix – industries (in the rows) by commodities (in the columns) – shows gross output of domestic industries by commodities;
- The absorption matrix – commodities by industries – shows intermediate consumption of domestic industries by commodities;
- The final demand matrix – commodities by categories of final demand – shows the final uses of commodities;
- And the value added matrix – components of value added by industries – shows the structure of value added of industries by components.

The final demand and value added matrix are conceptually the same as in the traditional input-output table of the Leontief type (quadrants II and III). However, the quadrant I (showing the inter-industry flows) is split up into two matrices, showing output and input separately (make matrix and absorption matrix). Quadrant I will only be the same as the absorption matrix in the extreme case where each industry produces only characteristic products. In practice non-characteristic output is the usual case. The attribution of the commodities used up in production of the different industries to the activities performed by them is a central task in compiling input-output tables, irrespective of whether SNA or MPS is the basis.

One of the main advantages of the make-use concept is that it allows the input and output data to be recorded exactly as they were originally observed. In the make matrices secondary output is entered in the off-diagonal elements; the absorption matrix shows all commodities used up in production both for the main output as well as for possibly secondary outputs. The make-use concept is, therefore, a good system for depicting the actual transactions in an economy.

The make-use matrices are the starting point for the derivation of "classical" input-output tables with symmetrical classifications (e.g. commodity by commodity) in the sense of the open Leontief model. Assumptions are then made on the technology of the different secondary outputs. The derivation procedure applied involves rearrangement of the absorption data in order to transfer commodities from intermediate consumption of those industries which have used them when producing their secondary output to the activities for which this secondary output is characteristic. The transformation of the make-use data to input-output matrices is a step of modelling. Here, the SNA proposes to use technology assumptions, of which the industry and the commodity technology are the extreme cases, but mixed (hybrid) technologies may also be assumed.

Usually, the basic data for the compilation of the national accounts are always to some extent incomplete and imperfect. There are classification problems and it may turn out that the data are inconsistent. On the basis of detailed and complete commodity accounts such problems will be seen more clearly and corresponding data correction can be done more easily. Accordingly, the use of the make-use approach will contribute to the quality of the national accounts estimates also. Only on that basis is there the possibility of cross-checking supply and use on a detailed level. It seems, therefore, advisable from the beginning to base the compilation of national accounts figures on a complete set of production and commodity accounts. In doing so one would at the same time achieve a make-use system to form the basis for the derivation of input-output tables as well as an integrated data system of national accounts and input-output as a whole.

There is another point that deserves attention, and this is the calculation of national accounts figures at constant prices (base year prices). Here again the make-use system provides an appropriate basis. Value added at constant prices is generally derived as the difference of gross output at constant prices minus intermediate consumption at constant prices ("double deflation method"). Since prices are only a property of commodities, one needs a breakdown both of gross output and intermediate consumption by commodities to apply price changes to the nominal values in order to deflate output and input. A complete elaborated make-use data system gives the data needed for constant price estimates.

Summing up, there are at least three reasons why the national accounts data system should be based on the make-use approach:

- Firstly, the make-use system forms a sound basis for deriving input-output tables. Compilation of input-output tables needs therefore not to be a separate task undertaken ex post for years for which national accounts figures are already existing, but could be elaborated simultaneously.
- Secondly, basing the compilation of national account figures on the concept of make-use contributes to the quality and consistency of the resulting estimates.
- Thirdly, make-use figures are a prerequisite for accurate constant price calculations.

Transition from MPS to SNA

Input-output is often used as a statistical frame for comparing MPS and SNA data. The differences between MPS and SNA become most obvious if an input-output data base is available. Usually, from the SNA tables the flows and activities of services not related to material production are extracted in order to obtain the production boundary concept valid in the MPS table. Therefore, the SNA make-use concept could also be used as a conceptual guideline to extend the MPS table according to the production boundary of the SNA.

Input-output tables according to the MPS are complete only as regards supply and use of material products. Material products used in non-material service activities are an entry in final demand as part of the consumption of the population. The transition from MPS to SNA requires, therefore, reallocation of these material products originally shown in final demand to intermediate consumption of the non-material service activities, which are included in the production boundary of the SNA.

In the transition from MPS to SNA one may start with the accounts of production, consumption and capital formation. The structure of these types of accounts can serve as a starting point in implementing the transition steps. The make-use system will support consistency between supply and use, and will allow cross-checks between the material products and the newly expanded service flows.

Development of basic statistics

It seems to be self-evident that the design of basic economic statistics should be oriented with a view to the structure and requirements of the national accounts. The transition from centrally-planned to market economies and the transition from MPS to SNA will change the structure and coverage of basic statistics in the CEECs in many ways. In the process of redesigning basic statistics the structure of the level I-accounts should serve as a guideline for the first steps. the following aspects are here relevant: statistical unit, structure of the reporting system, coverage, structure and definition of items surveyed.

The most important and also most difficult point is of course the question of the underlying statistical unit. Here, the application of the establishment concept will mean in most of the CEECs a total reorientation of their economic statistical system. Of course, production accounts could be compiled on the basis of enterprises, which is the prevailing statistical unit in the CEECs, but there would be a loss of homogeneity in the data shown by kind of economic activity, and the transformation of such data to input-output tables would remain a difficult task. There are two kinds of problems when an establishment basis is being set up: the one is the question of the availability of corresponding bookkeeping data, which may be less a statistical problem than a problem of general bookkeeping legislation. The other is the problem of developing and maintaining a business register which shows the changes of the existing enterprises, which will be very numerous due to the transition to a market economy, especially for small scale and self-employed activities (e.g. service sector). In such a register, the connections between enterprises and the establishments belonging to them have to be incorporated.

The production and commodity accounts provide guidelines regarding items to be surveyed, their definition and structuring. Regarding the first aspect, it is clear that data to be surveyed should include output, intermediate consumption, compensation of employees, gross fixed capital formation and stocks. The definition of the items should be in conformity with the SNA concepts. Regarding the structuring of the different items they should be designed such that relevant subtotals of the production accounts can be derived. Taking the items for gross output as an example, there should be separate items for production revenues and for trading activities so that it is possible to have basic data for estimating trade and transport margins. It is clear that it is not possible to incorporate a full commodity breakdown in all surveys. This will usually only be possible for certain activities and for large scale establishments. In the other cases it is therefore valuable to have at least some subtotal items available, for which a commodity breakdown could be estimated. Therefore, in the case of intermediate consumption the surveys should at least provide total data on energy consumption, on consumption of raw materials and other material inputs, on repair and maintenance inputs, on service inputs and so on. Regarding the general question of classifications it seems advisable to base the activity classification on ISIC, which in the coming version of Revision 3 is a very detailed and balanced activity classification. Any adaptation to ISIC, which may seem to be relevant from the national points of view, should be done in conformity with ISIC. The commodity classifications used in the surveys should therefore also be consistent with the activity classification. Every item of the commodity classification should have a one to one correspondence to an activity defined by ISIC. This is not only relevant for the surveys of output and input data, but also for the price statistics, whose data are a necessary input for constant price estimates.

IV. Input-output as an analytical instrument

As pointed out in the introduction it is not the intention to give a complete inventory of the analytical use of input-output in market economies. Instead, some examples of analytical use are listed which seem to be the most fruitful applications especially in the phase of transition to market economies. Input-output is an instrument which exhibits structural relations between factors of production (including intermediate consumption both of domestic and foreign origin) and final use of commodities. It is the special strength of input-output as an analytical instrument that both direct and indirect inter-industry relations are taken into account. Most of the input-output applications are based on the assumption of a Leontief production model, which assumes a proportional relationship between changes in the output level of an industry and the necessary changes in the direct inputs. This assumption is a plausible description of reality in the medium term analysis.

One of the standard input-output applications is the analysis between exports and the necessary direct and indirect inputs, of which imports seem to be of special interest (import content of exports). Such calculations show how much imports (directly and indirectly via inter-industry relations) are necessary for one unit of export broken down by the commodities shown in the input-output table. Thus, for every export commodity the necessary amount of foreign currency for the financing of the direct and indirect imports are shown. Such analysis will help in the question of export oriented policies.

The same kind of input-ouput approach can also be used for questions of analysing the effects of founding new industries/enterprises or closing existing ones. Not only the resulting effects on imports and exports will be of interest but also those affecting domestic production and employment.

Input-output is also a good instrument for the analysis of strategic input commodities. One of the most prominent example is energy. As in the case of import content cited above, one can calculate the energy content of the different commodities in final demand. Such an analysis can also be performed on the basis of physical energy data, which are to be calculated in the same way as the value data of the input-output table. Having such energy use matrices in physical terms (e.g. joules), the direct and indirect energy needs measured in physical terms can be calculated per unit of final demand.

One of the latest developments in input-output analysis is their use in environmental analysis. Several kinds of applications have been developed and applied in the analysis of the interrelations of economic process and environmental deterioration. Here, the input-output approach enables the determination of direct and indirect sources of pollution. For this, data on emission in physical terms have to be linked to the input-output tables. Based on the input-output calculus the pollution content of final demand can then be calculated. With such an enlarged data base, it is not only possible to estimate changes in the output levels of the industries due to changes in final demand, but also to estimate the resulting direct and indirect emissions due to the economic production activity. Empirical applications concentrate on important air pollutants such as sulphur dioxide, which is directly related to energy use. Therefore, energy input matrices in physical terms, as mentioned above, are an appropriate step also for environmental analysis.

Input-output can also be used for analysing changes in prices of the output of the industries resulting from changes in costs. The analytical approach here is the input-output price model. Based on this model one can answer the question: – What are the effects on the price level of the different final demand commodities of increases in import prices or in the costs of factors of production? A related application – of particular interest for CEECs – concerns subsidies. Input-output could show what changes in the price level of the industries (both those directly and indirectly involved) would result from reduction or elimination of subsidies.

Input-output is not only an instrument for exhibiting the structural relationships for a given year as it is described in the given input-output table. One can of course also do various kinds of sensitivity analysis (what will be the effects, if some variables in the input-output model are changed) or perform projections which show possibly future scenarios of the economy. For the latter kind of analysis input-output has to be integrated into a macro-economic (econometric) input-output model. Contrary to conventional macro-economic models a macro-economic input-output model takes into account the inter-industry flows explicitly. Therefore, the effects on domestic production due to changes in future final demand, which themselves may be based on regression analysis, can be calculated in a breakdown by industries. Here, of course, structural change in the input coefficients for future periods have to be modelled too. Such a model starts with the estimates for future final demand levels. Output and import levels to meet this final demand level are then calculated, further employment and income from production is determined, and output and final demand levels are linked in a consistent way. Well-known examples of such input-output models are the Cambridge model (United Kingdom) and the INFORUM models (United States and several other countries). They are mainly used for projections of the possibly future structure of an economy and for policy simulation purposes.

V

OECD Statistics: Selected Aspects

Economic Statistics Needed for OECD Country Reviews

Economics and Statistics Department

A main task of the OECD is to review the economic performance of its Member countries and forecast the likely developments in the year or so ahead. This paper describes the types of short-term statistics that are used in these reviews and also gives examples of the kinds of data used in structural adjustment studies.

I. Introduction

At approximately annual intervals, the OECD Secretariat prepares studies on the economies of each of its Member countries. These studies, which are carried out by the Economics and Statistics Department, are reviewed by the Economic and Development Review Committee (EDRC) which is composed of officials from Member countries. After revisions in the light of discussions during the review, the studies are published in the series *OECD Economic Surveys.*

These studies have traditionally served two purposes – to critically review each Member government's economic policies during the past year and to forecast the likely outturn of the economy during the coming 18 months. The review and forecasts concentrate on key aspects of macro-economic management and performance – in particular, on growth, inflation, unemployment and the current account balance. These studies are also used to monitor progress with "structural adjustment" and to assess the need for further micro-economic reforms. As used by the OECD, "structural adjustment" refers to changes in a country's economic institutions which may enhance "supply-side" efficiency. Examples of such changes include privatisation of state-owned firms, deregulation, tax-reform, reduction of subsidies and removal of barriers to trade and competition.

The next section of this note describes the kinds of economic statistics that are required for review of macro-economic performance and short-term forecasting. The last section briefly reviews the kinds of statistics needed for evaluating structural adjustment.

II. Types of data required for review of macro-economic performance

Table 1 lists the types of economic statistics that were used in the latest round (1989/90) of *OECD Economic Surveys.* The vertical columns show (by an "x")

Table 1. **Economic statistics used in 1989/90 "OECD economic surveys"**

	GERMANY	ITALY	AUSTRIA	DENMARK	GREECE	TURKEY	YUGOSLAVIA
NATIONAL ACCOUNTS (SNA)							
1. Final expenditure on GDP	x	x	x	x	x	x	x[1]
2. Income and outlay account: government	x	x	x	x	x	x[3]	x
3. Income and outlay account: households	x	x					x[2]
4. GDP by kind of activity	x	x	x	x	x	x	x
BALANCE OF PAYMENTS							
5. Current account	x	x	x	x	x	x	x
6. Capital account	x	x	x	x	x	x	x
7. Change in reserves	x	x	x	x	x	x	x
PRICES AND WAGES							
8. Consumer or retail price index	x	x	x	x	x	x	x
9. Producer or wholesale price index	x	x	x	x	x	x	x
10. GDP deflator	x	x	x	x	x	x	x
11. Export and import price indices	x	x	x	x	x	x	x
12. Compensation per employee	x	x	x		x		x
13. Hourly wage rates	x	x	x	x			
14. Unit labour costs	x	x	x	x	x		
LABOUR FORCE							
15. Employment	x	x	x	x	x	x	x
16. Unemployment	x	x	x	x	x	x	x
17. Vacancies	x			x			
MONEY AND INTEREST							
18. Money supply	x	x	x	x	x	x	x
19. Interest rates	x	x	x	x	x	x	x
OTHER ECONOMIC STATISTICS							
20. Industrial output indices	x	x	x	x	x	x	x
21. Capacity utilisation	x	x	x	x	x		
22. Business surveys	x	x	x	x	x		
23. Oil prices	x	x	x	x	x	x	x
24. Effective exchange rates	x	x	x	x	x	x	x
25. Labour productivity	x	x	x	x	x	x	

1. Current prices only.
2. According to MPS definitions.
3. Central government only.

countries for which the various statistics were available. Seven countries are shown: Germany and Italy which regularly publish a wide range of detailed economic statistics; Austria and Denmark which belong to the median group as regards data availability (although in recent months the latter has greatly expanded the coverage of its national accounts); Greece and Turkey which still have a number of data gaps; and Yugoslavia which may be most similar to the Central and Eastern European countries as regards the range of economic statistics available.

Statistics of *final expenditures on the GDP* (item 1) are central to the review and forecasting process. In OECD countries, short-term economic policy measures are mostly designed to act on the expenditure components of GDP – consumption, investment and the trade balance. Economic growth in the short-term is seen as being demand-driven and not supply-determined as in centrally-planned economies.

Data on final expenditure on the GDP are required at both current and constant prices because although current price data are of little interest in themselves there is considerable interest in the implicit price deflators obtained as ratios of current to constant price data.

Imports and exports need to be broken down both by partner countries and by broad commodity groups; this information is available for all OECD countries. Gross fixed capital formation should be broken down at least between the public and private sectors and, preferably, further subdivided by type of asset – dwellings, other buildings, machinery, etc. In practice, some countries are not able to distinguish between public and private capital formation and some can only classify capital formation according to industry of ownership.

The *income and outlay account for government* (item 2) is available for almost all OECD countries, although for Turkey this account is only compiled for the central (as opposed to general, i.e. total) government. This account shows the sources of government revenue – basically taxes and social security contributions – and the ways this revenue is spent – mainly on consumption, subsidies to industries and transfers to households. This account has a priority as high as that for final expenditure on the GDP.

The *income and outlay account for households* (item 3) provides information on two important variables – disposable income and saving. Several OECD countries are still not able to compile these accounts. In the case of Yugoslavia this account is available only according to the Material Product System (MPS).

GDP by kind of activity (item 4) is available for all countries. Most *OECD Economic Surveys* show the GDP decomposed into primary, secondary and tertiary sectors. Although shifts in the industrial composition of GDP are certainly of interest over long period they are of little interest for short term analysis. This table has a rather low priority.

The balance of payments (items 5 through 7) are high priority statistics and are available for all OECD countries. They are compiled according to the definitions and classifications of the IMF manual and distinguish between merchandise, factor services, non-factor services, and transfers in the current account balance, and between long and short-term transactions, in the capital account.

Price indices (items 8 through 11) are also high priority statistics and are available, in some form, for all OECD countries. Consumer and producer price indices are usually published for several sub-components – for example, "fuel and energy" and "food products" in the case of consumer price indices and "intermediate", "consumer" and "capital" goods in the case of producer price indices.

Price indices for exports and imports are often "unit value" indices. These are inferior to price indices in that the goods included in unit value indices are defined in very broad terms, so that the price changes recorded from one period to another may be due to differences in quality. Unit value indices are also affected by changes in the composition of the goods included in each commodity grouping. For these reasons some OECD countries are now replacing their unit value indices for imports and exports by proper price indices.

OECD countries attach great importance to the proper measurement of price changes, although they recognise the difficulties involved and are modest in claiming to have solved them all. Chief among these is the problem of adjusting for changes in quality. In particular, when a new "quality", "version" or "model" of an existing product is introduced at a higher price, efforts are made to *quantify* the quality change. Very often this means that the introduction of the new product results in an increase in the price index because the true value of the improvement in the quality of the new product is judged to be less than the increase in its price.

The simplest kind of *wage statistic* (items 12 through 14), is average compensation per employee, which is obtained by dividing the national accounts aggregate "compensation of employees" by the average number of employees. A narrower measure of the cost of labour is provided by statistics on hourly wage rates; several countries compile these data only for manufacturing industries. Unit labour costs are calculated by the OECD Secretariat as ratios of compensation of employees (at current prices) to value added (at constant prices).

Labour force statistics (items 15 through 17) are available for all countries although there are important quality differences between them. There is a general consensus among labour force statisticians that statistics on employment and, especially, unemployment should be based on household surveys. Employment statistics from surveys of establishments and unemployment statistics from administrative sources are inferior because they are necessarily less comprehensive. At the present time nearly three-quarters of OECD countries compile labour force statistics from household surveys.

Statistics on *money and interest rates* (items 18 and 19) are available for all OECD countries. The preferred measure of money supply is the broad "M3" definition, which includes time deposits as well as currency and checking accounts. All OECD countries publish a typical short-term (e.g. 3 months) and a long-term (e.g. 5 years) interest rate.

Most of the *other economic statistics* (items 20 through 25) are high priority series. Industrial output indices are widely available both in OECD countries and in Central and Eastern European countries. Their main interest for OECD analysts is that they provide up-to-date indicators of changes in GDP.

Capacity utilisation is one of the most important statistics collected through "business surveys". Business surveys are directed at owners or managers of enterprises and ask for their assessment of the current business climate and of prospects for the future. Business survey data are obviously valuable for short-term forecasting.

Oil prices and effective exchange rates are both calculated by the OECD Secretariat. The former is supplied by the International Energy Agency. The latter is an index which takes a country's base-year exchange rate against the currencies of its trade partners as 100.0 and measures the trade-weighted appreciation/depreciation of that country's currency since the base-year.

Labour productivity should be measured by comparing the change in value added to the change in labour inputs. Most countries have some measure of this kind though often it only covers manufacturing activities, output indices are often used instead of value added and numbers employed is often used as a proxy for labour inputs.

Two general points should be made in conclusion. First, although the *OECD Economic Surveys* give only *annual* statistics, the analysts who prepare the reports work with *monthly* or *quarterly* data whenever possible. These annual reports are in effect the outcome of a continuous, year-round monitoring process. Monthly or quarterly statistics on labour force, prices, output and, preferably, national accounts are thus essential for preparing an effective annual review.

Second, OECD analysts are mainly interested in the *demand* side of national accounts – consumption, investment and the trade balance. They almost never use input-output statistics nor the very detailed output indices that are typically published by Central and Eastern European countries.

III. Data needed for monitoring structural adjustment

The same types of statistics that are used for monitoring macro-economic policies are often also relevant for monitoring progress with structural adjustment. For the latter purpose, however, they need to be more disaggregated; for example, unemployment rates may need to be broken down by detailed age groups or by duration of unemployment, price indices may need to be broken down by detailed commodity groups, and employment statistics may need to be broken down by occupation and industry. So far as possible, the statistics used for structural adjustment studies should be compiled according to international standards to permit cross-country comparisons.

Some of the areas where the OECD Secretariat has investigated the need for structural adjustment are listed below, together with an indication of the kinds of statistics that may be considered relevant:

- **Industrial adjustment** (subsidies, profit shares, rates of return);
- **Labour markets** (unemployment benefits, replacement ratios, unit labour costs);
- **Financial markets** (cost of bond issues, income and cost margins of banks);
- **Distribution sector** (numbers of retail and wholesale outlets, employment in distribution, share of imports in consumption expenditure);
- **Public sector** (taxation, government debt, government transfer payments to households);
- **Environment** (consumption of fertilisers, vehicles per square kilometre, emission of hydrocarbons).

Leading Indicators: Applying the OECD System to Central and Eastern European Countries

Economics and Statistics Department

The OECD Secretariat has developed a set of "leading indicators" which can be used for predicting changes in the growth rate of industrial production. The paper describes the kinds of series that are typically used as leading indicators and how they are combined to form a composite index. The paper considers the possibility of applying the OECD Indicator System in Central and Eastern European countries. Most of these countries already publish several series that may serve as leading indicators but there is generally little data from "Business Surveys" which are widely used as leading indicators by OECD countries.

I. Introduction

Business cycle analysis is an area in which Central and Eastern European countries (CEECs) have little experience at present, but which is likely to become increasingly important as they move to market economies. The OECD Secretariat has developed a "leading indicator system" for its Member Countries which is used by the Secretariat and its Member countries for analysing business cycles and for predicting cyclical turning points. The first part of this note explains how the OECD leading indicators are calculated. The second part considers how similar methods could be used to calculate leading indicators for the CEECs.

II. The OECD system of leading indicators[1]

The reference series

The "reference series" is the economic variable whose cyclical movements it is intended to predict. Ideally, the OECD indicator system would use Gross Domestic Product (GDP) as the reference series, but for many countries GDP estimates are still available only on an annual basis and there is often a substantial time lag in their publication. Instead, the OECD indicator system uses the index of total industrial production – mining, manufacturing, utilities and construction – as the reference series. Indices of industrial production are available promptly for most Member countries and industrial production constitutes the more cyclical subset of the aggregate economy. In addition, the cyclical profiles of industrial production and Gross Domestic Product have been found to be closely related, so that the composite leading indicators for industrial production serve well as leading indicators for the GDP cycle.

Having identified the reference series, the next step is to determine its past cyclical behaviour. This is done by de-trending the series using the "Phase-Average-Trend" (PAT) method which is described below.

Selection of indicators

Once the underlying cyclical behaviour of the reference series has been established, the next step is to select economic time series whose cyclical movements typically predate those of the reference series. Candidate series are evaluated using the following criteria:

Relevance:

i) Economic significance – there has to be an economic reason for the observed leading relationship before the series can be accepted as an indicator;
ii) Breadth of coverage – series with a wide coverage, in terms of the representation of the economic activity concerned, are preferred to narrowly-defined series.

Cyclical behaviour:

iii) Length and consistency of the lead of the indicator over the reference cycle at turning points;
iv) "Cyclical conformity" between the indicator and the reference series – if the cyclical profiles are highly correlated, the indicator will provide a guide, not only to approaching turning points, but also to developments over the whole cycle;
v) Absence of extra or missing cycles in comparison with the reference series;
vi) Smoothness, that is, how promptly a cyclical turn in the series can be distinguished from irregular movements.

Practical considerations:

vii) Frequency of publication – monthly series are preferred to quarterly ones;
viii) Absence of excessive revisions;
ix) Timeliness of publication and easy accessibility for data collection and updating;
x) Availability of a long time series with no breaks.

To determine how well candidate series meet criteria three through six, two separate tests are carried out – a peak-and-trough analysis and a cross-correlation analysis.

For peak and trough analysis, statistics are assembled on each series' behaviour at cyclical turning points: the mean or median leads, the mean deviation from the median and the number of extra or missing cycles when compared with the reference series. Usually these figures are not statistically significant in the usual sense because of the limited number of turning points available over the period investigated, and because most series contain irregular movements and double or multiple peaks and troughs. Peak and trough analysis therefore involves a substantial amount of judgement. Cross-correlation analysis is used to complement the peak-and-trough analysis concerning the average lead of the indicator, and to give information about the extent to which the cyclical profiles of indicator and reference series resemble each other.

Certain practical factors – criteria seven through ten – need to be considered too, if the indicator system is to be updated regularly and used for current analysis of the economic cycle. These factors refer to matters of data collection, updating and computation, so that the final composite indicator can be calculated quickly and, as far as possible, automatically.

Leading indicators

The OECD system does not use a standard set of leading indicators for all countries, because of important differences between them in economic structure and statistical systems. Leading indicator series which perform well in both tracking and forecasting cyclical developments differ from country to country and may also change over time.

The different subject areas from which the leading indicator series are chosen are set out in Table 1. Certain types of series recur regularly in the list of leading indicators for different countries. Business survey series are among those most frequently used in the countries where they are available. These series concern business expectations on production, inflow of new orders, level of order-books, stocks of finished goods and the general economic situation. The most frequently used other series are monetary and financial series such as stock-market prices, money supply and interest rates. Series relating to stocks and orders, construction, retail sales, prices and foreign trade are also used frequently. Several series, such as stocks of finished goods, interest rates and prices, have to be inverted to obtain a positive correlation with the reference series.

Turning point and trend estimation

In common with most similar systems, the OECD leading indicator system uses the "growth cycle" or "deviation-from-trend" approach. This is necessary because essential cyclical similarities between series may be obscured by different long-term trends. Trend estimation is thus a crucial step in detecting cyclical movements and identifying turning points.

The method of trend estimation adopted by the OECD is a modified version of the Phase-Average Trend method developed by the United States National Bureau of Economic Research (NBER)[2]. This method has been designed specifically to separate the long-term trends from medium-term cycles, with the latter defined according to the criteria programmed in the Bry-Boschan computer routine[3] for selection of cyclical turning points.

Table 1. **Leading indicators used in the OECD system**

Indicator series by subject area	CANADA	USA	JAPAN	AUSTRALIA	AUSTRIA	BELGIUM	DENMARK	FINLAND	FRANCE	GERMANY	LUXEMBOURG	GREECE	IRELAND	ITALY	NETHERLANDS	NORWAY	PORTUGAL	SPAIN	SWEDEN	SWITZERLAND	UNITED KINGDOM	YUGOSLAVIA	ALL COUNTRIES
Production, stocks and orders																							
Industrial production in specific branches					1											1	2					1	5
Orders		1								1				1					1				4
Stocks – materials	1															1							2
– finished goods	1		1													2							4
– imported products																1							1
Ratios, e.g. inventory/shipment			1																				1
Construction, sales and trade																							
Construction approvals							1					1					1						3
Construction starts	1	1		1		1	1												1				6
Sales or registrations of motor vehicles	1						1		1									1			1		5
Retail sales							1					1	1		1							1	5
Labour force																							
Ratio new employment/employment																			1				1
Layoffs/initial claims, unemployment insurance		1																	1				2
Vacancies																						1	1
Hours worked	1												1										2
Prices, costs and profits																							
Wages and salaries per unit of output	1									1									1				3
Price indices		1							1			2			1	1							6
Profits, flow of funds, net acquisitions of financial assets																					2		2
Monetary and financial																							
Foreign exchange holdings								2															2
Deposits															1								1
Credit		1	1									1									1		4
Ratios, e.g. loans/deposits			1																				1
Money supply	1	1	1	1	1	1	1	1	1	1		1	1	1	1				1	1		1	17

Interest rates		1	1			1	1		3	1			1	1	1				1	1	1		14
Stock prices	1	1	1	1		1			1	1			1			1			1	1	1		12
Company formation		1																					1
Foreign trade																							
Exports aggregates																1							1
Exports components									2														2
Trade balance			1																				1
Terms of trade			1	1			1		1				1	1	1					1			8
Business surveys																							
General situation			1	1				1	1	1						1							6
Production	1			1	1	1	1	2	1			1		1	1	1		1		1	1		15
Orders inflow/new orders	1			1		1		1		1		1			1	1	1		1	1			11
Orderbooks/sales					1					1		1	1	1	1		1	2	1		1		11
Stocks of raw materials																	1		1		1		3
Stocks of finished goods	1		1						1	1			1	1	1				1	1	1		10
Capacity utilization																		2					2
Bottlenecks								1										1					2
Employment				1			1						1										3
Prices						1																	1
Economic activity in foreign countries	1				5						2				1								9
INDICATORS	12	9	11	8	9	7	9	10	11	9	2	9	9	7	11	11	6	7	12	7	10	4	190

The Phase-Average Trend (PAT) of a series is estimated by first splitting the series into *phases*, defined as the number of months between successive turning points. The means of the observations in each phase are then calculated and these *phase-averages* are used to compute a three-term moving average. The values obtained from the moving average are assigned to the mid-point of the three-phase period – known as a "triplet" – to which they refer. The trend is then obtained by computing the slope between the mid-point of successive triplets. The trend is extrapolated from the last available triplet to the end of the series by a least-squares log-linear regression starting from the mid-point of the last triplet.

It will be appreciated that the estimation of the peak and trough dates is a crucial step in the PAT procedure. First estimates are made using the Bry-Boschan routine, which begins by calculating a moving-average trend estimate for the identification of turning points. The routine then executes a series of tests on the deviations from this first trend estimate, so as to eliminate extreme values and turning points that are judged to be too close together; the Bry-Boschan routine specifies a minimum duration of five months for a phase and fifteen months for a cycle. These operations are applied to various smoothed curves in order to identify turning points which coincide more and more closely with observable variation in the original series. Last, the turning points are sought in the original series within the five months on both sides of the turning points found at the preceding stage. The points thus identified are taken as the preliminary turning points.

The main problem with the Bry-Boschan routine is that it tends to select too many turning points, thereby giving a long-term trend which is too variable; relatively minor fluctuations may be selected by the routine and given the same weight as more important cycles. The turning points finally chosen as input to the trend calculation are selected taking into account the relationship between the variables used in the indicator system. That is, care is taken to select the cyclical turning points corresponding to the reference chronology so that the trend estimation for each variable is done in a manner consistent with that for the other indicators and for the reference series itself. The same considerations apply in making the trend estimate for the reference series; here the main consideration is consistency between the turning points selected for a given country and the turning points for the other twenty-one countries included in the system.

Composite indicators

Once a set of leading indicators has been selected, they need to be combined into a single composite indicator for each country. This is done in order to reduce the risk of false signals, and to provide a leading indicator with better forecasting and tracking qualities than any of its individual components.

The reason why a group of indicators combined into a composite indicator should be more reliable over a period of time than any of its individual components is related to the nature and causes of business cycles. Each cycle has its unique characteristics as well as features in common with other cycles. But no single cause explains the cyclical fluctuation over a period of time in overall activity. The performance of individual indicators will then depend on the causes behind a specific cycle. Some indicators will perform better in one cycle and others in a different cycle. It is therefore necessary to have signals for the many possible causes of cyclical changes – i.e. to use all potential indicators as a group.

A number of steps are involved in combining individual series to obtain the composite indicator. First, the detrended indicator series are all converted to a monthly basis. Most indicators used in the OECD system are in fact monthly series, but it is sometimes necessary to accept quarterly data. These are converted to monthly frequency by linear interpolation.

Next, it is necessary to ensure that all component series have equal "smoothness"; this is to ensure that month-to-month changes in the composite indicator are not unduly influenced by irregular movements in any one indicator series. The OECD procedure is to use the "Months for Cyclical Dominance" (MCD) moving average[4]. This procedure ensures approximately equal smoothness between series, and also ensures that the month-to-month changes in each series are more likely to be due to cyclical than to irregular movements.

The third step is to normalise the series so that their cyclical movements have the same amplitude; if this were not done series with particularly marked cyclical amplitude would have undue weight in the composite indicator. The method used to calculate normalised indices is, for each component series, to first subtract the mean and then divide by the mean of the absolute values of the differences from the mean. The normalised series are then converted into index form by adding 100.

Finally, it may sometimes be necessary to lead or lag particular indicators. In the OECD system this is done only in one case, where the indicators selected for a particular country fall into two distinct groups of "longer-leading" and "shorter-leading" indicators. Combining the two types of indicators gave unsatisfactory results because of the interference between the two cycles. The alignment was improved by lagging the longer-leading group of indicators.

The indicator series, having been detrended, converted to a monthly basis, smoothed, normalised and, possibly, lagged to improve alignment, are now ready to be combined into a single composite indicator. At this stage it would be possible to assign different weights to the component series depending, for example, on their past record in forecasting and tracking cycles or on their relative freedom from revisions. In the OECD system, equal weights are used almost invariably to obtain each country's composite indicator; this does not mean that there is "no weighting" in the OECD system, because equal weighting implies, by default, a judgement on appropriate weights, and the normalisation process is itself a weighting system in reverse. However, when the composite indicators for individual countries are combined into indicators for country groups, each composite indicator is assigned the weight used in calculating group totals for the industrial production index.

III. A system of leading indicators for Central and Eastern European Countries

Selection of reference series

The only series available on a monthly basis for all CEECs is the total industrial production index. If a single economic variable is to be used as reference series for a leading indicator system in CEECs, total industrial production index is obviously the best candidate.

Total industrial production (ISIC 2,3,4) includes extractive industry and public utilities which may distort the general pattern of the reference cycle. If this should be the case, manufacturing production (ISIC 3) could be used instead.

Potential leading indicators

The first criteria used when evaluating potential leading indicators is economic significance. There must be an economic reason for the observed leading relationship before the series can be accepted as an indicator.

Leading indicators can be classified according to five types of "economic rationale"[5]:

i) Early stage indicators;
ii) Rapidly responsive indicators;
iii) Expectation-sensitive indicators;
iv) Prime movers;
v) Other indicators.

The first category contains indicators which measure an early stage of production. The second contains indicators which respond rapidly to changes in economic activity. The third covers indicators which measure expectations or are sensitive to expectations. The fourth contains measures relevant to monetary and fiscal policies and foreign economic developments. The fifth category contains indicators of mixed types such as interest rates (stimulus to both consumption and investment), overtime and layoff rate and production in specific branches.

For the 22 countries included in the OECD indicator system, the total number of indicators are rather evenly split between the different categories. *Early stage* indicators, *expectation-sensitive* indicators and *prime movers* represent around 20 per cent each of the total number of indicators. *Rapidly responsive* indicators represent around 14 per cent, while *other indicators* represent about 28 per cent of the total.

In three of the categories – *early stage, rapidly responsive* and *expectation-sensitive* indicators – business surveys provide most of the series used. These series concern new orders, level of order-books and stocks and expectations about production. Two other frequently used series in these categories are construction approvals or starts and stock prices.

The most important series used in the *prime movers* category is money supply. Two series related to foreign trade and foreign economic developments are also well represented in this category, namely, terms of trade and indicators for foreign countries.

Among the *other indicators*, the most frequently used series are different types of interest rates. Series on production in specific branches and series related to retail sales or motor vehicles registration are also frequently used.

Differences between countries in choice of indicators are, however, important. Available statistics and economic structure make it hard to find a common set of indicators for all countries. In the category, *rapidly responsive* indicators, no good indicators have been found for eight countries (United States, Australia, Austria, Belgium, Denmark, Luxembourg, Greece and Yugoslavia). For three countries (Japan, France and Luxembourg) no early stage indicators have been found and in the category expectation-sensitive indicators three countries are also missing (Luxembourg, Portugal and Yugoslavia). *Prime movers* are also missing for three countries (Portugal, Spain and the United Kingdom), while only one country (Luxembourg) is missing in the category *other indicators.*

Existing indicators for CEECs are set out in Table 2 using the classification by type of rationale. This, of course, is based on the assumption that a series which is a leading indicator for OECD countries is a potential leading indicator for CEECs as well.

In the category *early stage* indicators, construction starts is available for several countries and a series on vacancies is published by Poland. This leaves Romania as the only country with no series in this category. The only *rapidly responsive* indicator is a series on average hours worked. This is available in the Czech and Slovak Federal Republic, Poland and Romania. *Expectation-sensitive* indicators are not available for any country, while prime movers are better represented. In this category, money supply is available for three countries (Hungary, Poland and Romania) and export indicators available for all countries with the exception of Romania and the USSR. A series on deposits is also available for the Czech and Slovak Federal Republic. In the category, *other indicators*, three or more indicators are available for all CEECs. The different indicators are found among production series for specific branches or commodities, retail sales, interest rates and foreign trade balance.

Development of new indicators

The previous section has tried to identify potential leading indicators from among the short-term statistics published in CEECs. This exercise has shown a lack of indicators in three categories: *early stage* indicators, *rapidly responsive* indicators and *expectation-sensitive* indicators. The easiest way to improve this situation would be to set up business surveys to collect information on new orders, order-books, stocks and production expectations.

In the area of *prime movers*, series on terms of trade and indicators for foreign countries could be developed. Money supply series could also be improved or developed. The coverage of *other indicators* could be improved by developing more employment indicators, price indices, motor vehicle registration series and interest rates series.

Data needs and cyclical analysis

The comments above are based on the assumption that the OECD leading indicator system is applicable to the CEECs. No data analysis has been carried out to test this assumption.

In order to identify the cyclical behaviour of the reference series and of the potential leading indicator series, data must be available on a monthly or quarterly basis for a period of at least 6 years. This is necessary in order to carry out seasonal

Table 2. **Indicators for CEECs classified by type of rationale**

Indicators by type of rationale	Bulgaria	Czecho-slovakia	German Democratic Republic	Hungary	Poland	Romania	USSR	All countries
Early stage indicators								
New orders, amounts								
New orders (BS)								
Orderbooks (BS)								
Construction, approvals/starts	1	1	1	1			1	5
New company formation								
Vacancies					1			1
Total: number	1	1	1	1	1	0	1	6
percent								12
Rapidly responsive indicators								
Average hours worked		1				1	1	3
Profits								
Stocks, amounts								
Stocks (BS)								
Production bottlenecks (BS)								
Total: number	0	1	0	0	1	1	0	3
per cent								7
Expectation-sensitive indicators								
Stock prices								
Raw material prices								
Selling prices (BS)								
Production (BS)								
Economic situation (BS)								
Total: number	0	0	0	0	0	0	0	0
per cent								0
Prime movers								
Money supply								
Deposits				1	1	1		3
Exports		1						1
Terms of trade		1	1	1	1	1		5
Indicators for foreign countries								
Total: number	1	2	1	2	2	1	0	9
per cent								22
Other indicators								
Production in specific branches	1	1	1	1	1	1	1	7
Retail sales	1	1	1	1	1	1	1	7
Motor vehicle registrations							1	1
Layoffs/new hire/claims for unemployment insurance								
Price indices		1						1
Unit labour costs								
Credit ratios								
Interest rates				1	1	1		3
Foreign exchange holdings								
Foreign trade balances	1	1	1	1	1			5
Capacity utilisation (BS)								
Employment situation (BS)								
Total: number	3	4	3	4	4	3	3	24
per cent								59
Grand total: number	5	8	5	7	8	5	4	41
per cent								100

1. Items marked (BS) are series derived from business surveys.

adjustments and to detect cyclical movements. Two problems may arrive in connection with this. First, there may be statistical breaks in the data between the pre and post-transition periods. Second, even if there are no breaks of a statistical nature, there may be fundamental differences in the mechanisms of economic growth in the two periods; relationships discovered between the reference series and leading indicators in the pre-transition period may no longer apply after transition.

A final caveat: leading indicators are normally used to monitor cyclical fluctuations in *real* output and to do this it is essential to use, as far as possible, series adjusted for inflation. This means that it is necessary to have reliable price deflators as well as a broad range of leading indicators.

Notes and References

1. This part is based on Ronny Nilsson, OECD (1987) "OECD Leading Indicators", *Economic Studies No. 9.*
2. United States National Bureau of Economic Research. The method is described in BOSCHAN, Charlotte and EBANKS, Walter (1978), "The Phase-Average Trend, a New Way of Measuring Economic Growth", *Proceedings of the Business and Economic Statistics Section,* American Statistical Association.
3. BRY, Gerhard and BOSCHAN, Charlotte (1971), "Programmed turning point determination" in *Cyclical Analysis of Time Series: Selected Procedures and Computer Programmes*, NBER.
4. Months for Cyclical Dominance. MCD is defined as the shortest span of months for which the I/C ratio is less than unity. I and C are the average month-to-month changes without regard to sign of the irregular and trend-cycle component of the series, respectively. Although I remains approximately constant as the span of months increases, C should increase, thus the I/C ratio, itself a measure of smoothness, should decline, and eventually become less than unity. In practice there are some series for which the I/C ratio at first declines as the span in months increases, then starts to increase again without ever having dropped as low as 1. Thus, there is a convention that the maximum value of MCD should be 6. For quarterly series there is an analogous measure, Quarters for Cyclical Dominance (QCD), which has a maximum value conventionally defined as 2.
5. This 5-way classification is taken from DE LEEUW, Frank (1989), "Leading Indicators and the 'Prime Mover View'", *Survey of Current Business,* US Department of Commerce.

Energy Statistics

International Energy Agency

The International Energy Agency compiles statistics on the global supply and use of energy so it already collects some energy statistics for Central and Eastern European countries. The paper describes the additional detail that will be required for these countries to participate fully in the Agency's regular statistical programme. A more detailed set of statistics is required for reviews of energy policies in individual countries and for studies of the environmental impact of energy production and use.

I. Introduction

The collection of statistics relating to energy supply and use in Central and Eastern European countries (CEECs) is a part of the International Energy Agency's overall energy information gathering exercise covering countries which are not members of the OECD. Over the past five years a data base has been constructed which comprises 84 individual non-OECD countries which taken together represent over 98 per cent of non-OECD energy requirements. In building up the data base priority has been given to data obtained from government ministries and agencies. This material has been supplemented with the "World Energy Supplies" data base of the United Nations and with data collected by the Economic Commission for Europe (ECE).

Data thus obtained have occasionally been adjusted or estimated after consultations with industry – especially with international oil and energy companies. Their comments allow us to reconcile, refine and expand our data sources. In the case of the statistics of CEECs, most of the data are obtained through ECE channels and direct contact with statistical bodies or ministries in CEECs.

II. Scope of data collection

The data the International Energy Agency (IEA) seeks to obtain, in the first instance, are those covering the volume of commonly traded fuels and the prices of certain key transactions. Statistics of energy commodities are presented in the well known commodity balance format in which the balance between supply and use of the fuels is set out with each element of supply and use identified to the maximum extent possible. Our aim is to obtain from CEECs (and non-OECD countries in general), commodity balances for each fuel product with the timeliness and accuracy provided by most OECD Member countries. The extent to which this can be realised depends on the availability of the data in each individual country as well as the part of the balance (e.g. whether coal, electricity or oil; whether supply, transformation or end use) being considered.

In general sufficient detail of supply and demand can be obtained for CEECs on an annual basis although the time in the year when the data are available varies between countries. Supply data are usually published with greater frequency, (monthly or quarterly) than demand data but their consistency with later annual information is not always good. Among the supply elements it is especially difficult to obtain rapid and reliable trade data on the basis of physical movements of fuels across frontiers (it is desirable to exclude "paper" trade from reported import and export data). It is particularly difficult to arrive at reliable trade data if good product differentiation is required. Moreover, until recently, no CEEC had adopted fully the international trade classification for external trade in fuels.

Full detail on the demand side of fuels, especially oil products, has not hitherto been available for CEECs. Often very little information below the level of total energy requirements was available. An important task in the future will be to complete the demand side of the balance in as much detail as possible. The IEA requests OECD countries to provide it with consumption data for over twenty five individual fuel categories for more than thirty end use sectors (including transformation and energy sectors).

Recent co-operative work instituted by the ECE means that the ECE, the IEA and EUROSTAT (the statistical office of the European Communities) have adopted a set of common questionnaires for the annual reporting of oil, gas electricity and coal and manufactured gases from their respective member countries. This will assist reporting on the basis of a common set of definitions and methodology and will improve the quality and comparability of the statistics. It should also help to reduce the reporting burden of respondents.

III. Use of the statistics

The IEA maintains an energy statistics system in order to support activities which include the following:

- Preparedness for oil emergencies;
- Monitoring of energy markets, especially oil markets;
- Promotion of energy efficiency;
- Review of OECD national energy policies;
- Pursuit of energy research and development;
- Study of fiscal and financial aspects of energy developments;
- Identification of issues related to energy and the environment; and
- Dissemination of information on energy matters.

In the case of CEECs the IEA, until recently, restricted energy data gathering efforts to compiling annual supply and demand balances for the main fuels. This was felt to be the most that could be reasonably achieved given the difficulty in obtaining reliable energy statistics, particularly oil statistics in these countries. With the new climate, the IEA hopes to widen the scope of data it collects for CEECs and has focused its expanded data gathering in the areas outlined below.

Oil markets

The statistics of fuel use in the CEECs collected by the IEA are used to support the ongoing broad activities of the Agency outlined above and which existed before the fundamental changes in Central and Eastern Europe took place. Recently of course there has been considerable new demand for energy statistics of the CEECs to support analyses of the energy economies of these countries.

As a by-product of monitoring the international oil market the IEA publishes each month its "Monthly Oil Market Report". This sets out to analyse the regional elements of world oil supply and demand. To date data of adequate quality were not available for CEECs that would permit them to be shown on both the supply and demand sides of the oil balance. Instead these countries were included under a heading of Net Exports of Centrally-Planned Economies (CPEs).

The IEA has since its inception been able to monitor the extent of what used to be called "CPE trade" with the OECD (OECD countries are obliged to report trade data to the IEA on a monthly basis). However, the IEA has always experienced great difficulty in quantifying CPE trade with the non-OECD region and consequently this has been one of the most uncertain elements in the world oil balance.

We expect in future that the role of CEECs will become more important in the world oil market as they are likely to purchase oil from a variety of international sources. For these reasons it will be necessary for the IEA to expand its data for CEECs to include adequate data on oil trade flows – if possible on a monthly or quarterly basis. Indeed the effort to obtain more reliable oil trade statistics on CEECs has high priority in the IEA.

Energy and environment

The effects on the environment of energy production, distribution and use is a sensitive subject for all countries and likely to remain so indefinitely. The high political profile given to environmental matters means that many of the IEA's member countries wish to see the IEA play an important role in carrying over to the CEECs the knowledge the Agency is gaining through its close examination of emission control options of all types, their economic effects and political value. The work is now moving beyond its initial "broad brush" stage to more precisely targeted studies of individual fuel consuming sectors and the emission reduction options available to each.

Clearly the applicability of the results of these studies to CEECs cannot be even considered without the essential data provided by the fuel product commodity balance. The provision of sufficiently detailed energy data for sectorial studies of environmental effects in OECD countries is a taxing and not always successful venture. We are not yet at the stage where similar data are available for the CEECs. Nevertheless the OECD studies allow the IEA to suggest methods of approach and the corresponding data requirements to the CEECs which approach it for advice.

In order to monitor and analyse changes and trends in energy and environmental matters, data on energy infrastructure will need to be collected on a systematic basis. Data on power station characteristics (capacity, fuel use, etc.), on fuel specifications (sulphur content, vapour pressure, etc.), vehicle fleet characteristics (average fuel efficiency by engine size, etc.) are just some of the data which will be needed.

Review of energy policies and programmes

A number of CEECs have expressed interest in hearing the IEA's view of their energy economies, their balance of fuels used, their plans for the future development of electricity generation, their exploitation of natural energy resources, the scope for energy efficiency in different sectors, the scope for energy conservation and other issues. These matters are discussed regularly and critically reviewed, for each IEA country in turn by its peers in an annual review process.

Some CEECs have suggested that a similar review be conducted for their countries, either in its entirety or for certain fuel or economic sectors. Once again such studies presume a good base of statistics covering far more than the volume figures that are the majority of our statistical collection. To conduct this work a certain amount of information on the energy industry infrastructure is required. The first approaches in this direction have been made with the sending of the inevitable questionnaire to gather the detail normally collected for these studies.

In addition to volume data on supply and demand for fuels, the IEA requests data, from its member countries, on the following topics for historical, current and forecast periods. The forecast horizon is usually ten years.

- End use efficiency indicators in transport, industry, residential and commercial/public sectors;
- Public sector budgets for improving end-use efficiency by sector;
- Oil and gas exploration and development (metres drilled, wells completed offshore and onshore, etc.);
- Proven reserves of oil, coal and gas;
- Contribution of renewables (solar, wind, etc., to energy supply);
- Planned electricity by fuel;
- Information on government and industry energy research and development budgets classified by fuel and purpose.

IV. Conclusion

Statistical agencies in CEECs may find the scope of these statistics very wide and difficult to provide especially if they are in the throes of restructuring. However the types of energy statistics identified are those which the IEA believes are the first requirement for conducting analyses of energy policy and programmes. As such they may be useful in helping CEECs identify data priorities in their transition phase to market economies.

Government Revenue Statistics

Directorate for Financial, Fiscal and Enterprise Affairs

This paper explains how taxes are defined in OECD statistics, describes the numerous borderline issues that arise and explains how they have been resolved. The "tax-burden" – taxes as a percent of GDP – is a statistic with important economic and political implications in OECD countries, but it needs to be carefully interpreted when used as an indicator of levels of government intervention or of resource transfers from private to public sectors.

I. Introduction

The purpose of the OECD classification of taxes is to provide internationally comparable data on tax levels and structures in Member countries of the OECD. The taxes of each country, including social security contributions, are presented in a standardised framework based upon the *OECD Classification of Taxes and Interpretative Guide* (OECD).

In drawing up this classification, the work of other organisations in this field has also been taken into account. The most important of the other classifications currently in use are the United Nations System of National Accounts (SNA), and the European System of Integrated Economic Accounts of the European Communities (ESA), which is primarily an elaboration of SNA. There is no incompatibility between these classifications and the OECD one and SNA/ESA figures can be derived from figures in the OECD list and SNA criteria and definitions have been adopted unless the contrary is specifically indicated.

The tax data have been published annually since 1973 in the OECD publication *Revenue Statistics of OECD Member Countries*. This series was established to throw light on such questions as: how do countries' tax burdens compare; what are the economic effects of different tax levels; what is the relative reliance on different sources of revenue; what, if any, is the significance of such differences for economic performance. Data on tax levels and structures can also provide insights into the scope for tax reform in a particular country.

The OECD classification first distinguishes between taxes and non-tax revenues such as user charges, capital sales and fee. It then classifies the taxes according to the base upon which they are levied – income and profits, payroll, property, goods and services, other – and, in some cases, according to who pays contributions – households, companies, institutions. With the exception of social security contributions – a separate heading in the OECD list – "earmarking", i.e., the purpose for which the tax is levied, does not affect classification. To ensure international comparability, detailed guidelines are laid down as to what counts as a tax, and where revenues from specific taxes should be classified. Before the results are published, the country submissions are verified to ensure that country returns conform to the guidelines.

II. What is a tax?

Definition problems

Unlike elephants, which are easy to recognise but difficult to define, taxes are difficult both to define and to identify. The OECD interpretative guide defines a tax as follows: "the term taxes is **confined to compulsory**, **unrequited** payments to **general government**". To formulate these criteria took many hours of debate among statisticians and tax specialists. Even if the amount of revenue (and hence international comparability) is not greatly affected in most of the borderline cases encountered, fundamental points of principle are involved. Each of the emphasised words in this definition of taxes poses problems:

a) "**Confined to**": There may be levies which are compulsory, unrequited payments to general government, but which it is preferred not to regard as taxes. One example is compulsory loans to government which have occurred in some countries.

b) "**Compulsory**" is not without ambiguity, as can be seen by examining the following three areas:

Contributions paid to social security funds. For the most part, social security contributions are compulsory in the everyday sense that the payers have no choice as to whether or not they contribute. In practice, however, it can be difficult to distinguish between compulsory and quasi-compulsory contributions. For example:

- Under certain social security schemes (e.g. Dutch health insurance), contributions are compulsory up a certain income level and then become optional. In this case, the contributions paid by the taxpayers below the ceiling are treated as taxes, but those paid above the ceiling are considered to be voluntary and are not treated as taxes;
- In some countries (e.g. the United Kingdom), employers have the choice of contributing to a public pension scheme or setting up a private scheme which provides at least the same level of benefits. Contributions to the public schemes are regarded as compulsory, but represent a borderline case.

Even where conceptually the treatment of these contributions may seem fairly self-evident, there remains the problem that is not always easy to identify what amounts are in practice compulsory and what voluntary.

Levies paid to the church. A number of North European countries have levies which are earmarked for the church. Where these levies are paid by nearly all citizens and the church is part of general government, they are treated as taxes. In most cases, however, these levies are compulsory only for those citizens who belong to the church, though the presumption is that everybody is a church-member unless they expressly opt out. And opting out can involve the citizen in a lot of effort.

Fees which are paid for certain services provided by government. Problems arise as to whether or not certain fees are compulsory. A fee paid to obtain a passport, for example, is compulsory only for those who intend to travel abroad, which is a "voluntary" decision. In practice, fees of this kind seem generally designed broadly to cover administrative costs rather than to raise revenue, and are generally regarded in the OECD classification as not being taxes. In a few countries (e.g. Portugal), where there is a deliberate revenue-raising element, usually by way of a surcharge on the passport fee, they are taken to be taxes.

c) "**Unrequited**" is used in the sense that benefits provided by government to a taxpayer are not in proportion to the payments made by that taxpayer. Many borderline cases arise with regard, for example, to passport fees, driving licences, and licences for public radio and television services, where it is difficult to decide whether they should be treated as taxes or as non-tax revenues. An attempt to make this distinction has been made in the interpretative guide to the OECD Revenue Statistics and the amounts of revenues affected by any remaining incomparabilities are likely to be small. In the national accounts these fees are treated as taxes when paid by enterprises and as non-tax revenues when paid by households. Tax administrations tend to take the view that such fees are generally not intended to raise revenue but to cover costs and so should not be regarded as taxes. For the most part, the OECD treatment follows the latter point of view, borderline cases being resolved by reference to the general practice of tax administrations.

d) "**General government**" also provides problems. In the OECD classification, general government consists of supra-national authorities (in practice, the Commission of the European Communities), the central administration and the agencies whose operations are under its effective control, state and local governments and their administrations, social security schemes and autonomous governmental entities, excluding public enterprises. One problem is that in some countries (e.g. Finland) the church is considered as part of government and performs certain services for government, such as registration of marriages. Yet it is questionable whether the church is "effectively under the control" of government. A second problems arises with separate social security agencies. For the most part, separate social security funds are clearly within general government but some funds are regulated by government though administered by the private sector. Some countries have separate funds for certain professions (e.g. Italy for doctors) where the control effectively rests with the profession, though the funds have to operate within the framework established by legislation. In practice, separate social security agencies of this kind are treated as part of general government.

Should social security contributions be regarded as taxes?

The problems discussed above raise important conceptual issues, but chosen solutions do not greatly affect international comparability of tax revenues. The treatment of social security contributions is much more important in this regard.

Examples have already been cited where certain types of social security contributions fit uneasily with the definition of taxes because they are not really compulsory or not unrequited or not paid to general government. They have also special features which make them arguably non-tax revenues:

- They are the only major source of revenue which is earmarked for a particular purpose;
- Contributions provide an entitlement to benefits and could therefore be considered as requited;
- Because of the insurance analogy, they may be perceived differently from other revenues by governments, politicians, employers and employees.

Nevertheless, it would be inappropriate to exclude compulsory social security contributions in international comparisons of tax levels, because countries rely to differing degrees on them to finance similar kinds of social benefits. For example, in France, Italy, the Netherlands and Spain social security contributions amount to more than 40 per cent of tax revenues, whereas they are less than three per cent in Denmark, and zero in Australia and New Zealand. Moreover, there exists the borderline case in the Nordic countries (other than Sweden) of levies on employees which could be regarded as either an income tax earmarked for social security contributions (to be classified as an income tax) or as social security contributions levied on an income tax base (to be classified as social security contributions). The OECD has classified such levies as income taxes.

The borderline between tax provisions and direct government expenditures

There are two areas where it is difficult to distinguish between tax provisions and direct government expenditures and where, because the amounts of revenue are considerable, the choice made would significantly affect countries' ranking order in tax level comparisons. One is the case of investment and savings premiums. These are subsidy programmes administered by the tax authorities and which can, under certain conditions, be subtracted from tax due, such as the investment premiums which were used in Austria, Germany and the Netherlands.

The second difficult area is the treatment of "non-wastable" tax credits. In most countries, tax credits are "wastable" in the sense that any excess over the liability is not refunded to the taxpayer. These credits are treated as tax provisions since they affect the flow of receipts to governments and are an integral part of tax assessment process. In a few countries (e.g. Canada, New Zealand, France, the United States) there are non-wastable tax credit which can be offset against tax liability and any excess of the credit of tax liability is paid out to the taxpayer. The question arises of how should the payments of the excess credit be treated. After discussion in the OECD it was decided that the amount of credit offset against tax should be treated as a tax provision, thus reducing tax receipts, but that payments made by governments should be regarded as a direct government expenditure provision and so would not affect tax receipts. However, arguments can be put forward for treating non-wastable tax credits, both as entirely tax provisions and as entirely government expenditure.

III. Difficulties in interpreting data

Ratios of taxes to GDP are commonly used to compare **tax burdens** between countries. However, these ratios must be interpreted with care and this section argues that they cannot provide an unequivocal guide either to the level of government intervention in the economy or to the level of compulsory transfers from the private to the public sector.

Various means of government intervention

In OECD countries, governments intervene in the economy in the following ways:

- Direct government expenditures. This may be financed by taxes, non-tax revenues or by borrowing;
- Tax expenditures. As discussed below, there are subsidy programmes implemented via the tax system which have the effect of reducing tax revenues below what they would otherwise have been;
- Government loan guarantees. These reduce the cost of borrowing below what it would otherwise be;
- An obligation on the private sector to collect compulsory levies for the provision of certain social security benefits. The amounts represent between 4 to 6 per cent of GDP in Finland, the Netherlands, and Switzerland;
- Other government regulatory activities which increase the costs of the private sector (e.g. environmental control);
- There are various means by which a government can extract revenue from a particular activity. For example, if the government wishes to obtain more revenue from the activity of gambling it can do so either through the tax route (a tax on the betting stake or the net profits or gross turnover of the gambling enterprise) or the non-tax route of a State lottery: if it wishes to raise extra money from electricity consumption it can do so by an indirect tax or by the non-tax route of increasing the price of electricity supplied by a nationalised industry and requiring that industry to transfer part of the increased revenue to general government.

Relative reliance on tax expenditures and direct expenditures

Perhaps the single most important difficulty in interpreting published tax burden comparisons is that one country may place a heavy reliance on tax expenditures – subsidies paid out via the tax system – whilst another may rely predominantly on direct expenditures to achieve its policy goals. Other things being equal, the tax level of a country in the first category will be lower than that of a country in the second category, even if in the two cases, the level of government intervention in the economy and the resource cost are similar. A conceptual complication is that there is room for disagreement on whether particular provisions, such as tax allowances for parents, or lower rates of value-added tax, should be regarded as a tax expenditure which is a substitute for a direct expenditure or as an integral part of the tax structure. In any event, only about half of OECD countries can provide data on these tax expenditures and the data available are unlikely to be fully comparable on an international basis.

Taxes paid by government to itself

Taxes paid by government to itself constitute a relatively large and varying proportion of government receipts, taking the form either of payments from one level of government to another – for example, local property taxes paid by central government – or of payments by the same level of government to itself, such as VAT payments on purchases by central government. Two questions arise:

- Can the amounts of revenue in question be isolated and what is their relative importance?
- If identifiable, should they be included or excluded from tax statistics?

With regard to the first question, it seems that the most important of these levies are social security contributions paid by government in their capacity as employers and the amounts involved can usually be identified. These can be very sizeable, amounting in the extreme case of Sweden to nearly 5 per cent of GDP. Few governments can identify the amounts of property or consumption taxes they pay to themselves: extrapolating from those that can, the amounts seem relatively slight in comparison to payments of social security contributions.

Opinions vary as to whether identifiable amounts of taxes paid by government to itself should be eliminated from tax receipts. OECD has decided against elimination, and IMF for elimination (and this constitutes the only conceptual difference between the data provided by the two Organisations). The argument for elimination is that if the intent is to provide data on the flow of cash payments to the government sector from the rest of the economy, then tax payments between different units of the same level of government, and between different levels of government, should be eliminated in the consolidation of the tax accounts of general government. This treatment also has the advantage that differing country practices, as regards the exemption from tax of similar government activities, does not distort inter-country comparisons. On the other hand, if the aim of recording tax flows is to provide an insight into the value of government output in the context of the economy as a whole, then the appropriate treatment is to take into account payments by government. This treatment ensures that the different resource flows of an economy, including the valuation of the output of government, are measured consistently. Consistency would also require that imputed tax payments are calculated when a government activity is exempt from a tax that would have applied if the activity was carried out in the private sector. Another argument against elimination is that it is anyway in practice impossible to eliminate all such payments by government to itself and that the proportion of such payments which cannot be eliminated will vary from country to country.

Purchasing Power Parities

Economics and Statistics Department

The OECD and EUROSTAT jointly calculate purchasing power parities (PPPs) for all 24 Member countries of the OECD. To participate in this programme, national statistical offices must provide detailed statistics on final expenditures on the GDP and prices for a basket of carefully defined goods and services. The paper describes how the goods and services are selected, how their price are measured and how they are used to calculate PPPs. At present, PPPs are only calculated every five years. Together with Eurostat, the OECD Secretariat is devising procedures for annual updating.

I. Introduction

The **EUROSTAT-OECD Purchasing Power Parity (PPP) Programme** was established in the early 1980s to enable international price and volume comparisons of GDP and its component expenditures to be made for OECD Member countries. The comparisons are multilateral comparisons based on a matrix of binary comparisons, that is, each country is compared directly with each of the other participating countries.

To date, the Programme has provided benchmark PPPs for 1980 and 1985 using price and expenditure data collected in the intervening years. Final benchmark PPPs for 1990 are expected to be available in early 1992 after the current cycle of price and expenditure surveys is completed. Eighteen countries participated in the 1980 exercise and 22 countries participated in the 1985 exercise. All 24 Member countries are participating in the 1990 exercise.

As its name implies, the Programme is jointly organised by EUROSTAT (the Statistical Office of the European Communities) and the OECD. The countries co-ordinated by EUROSTAT, or "EUROSTAT countries", are the 12 Community countries plus Austria and Switzerland. The countries co-ordinated by the OECD, or "OECD countries", are the four Nordic Member countries, Turkey and the five non-European Member countries. Links between the two groups of countries are provided by the OECD. Benchmark calculations, both for the European Communities and for the OECD as a whole, are made by EUROSTAT in the first instance.

II. Main features of the programme

Breakdown of expenditures and product selection

The calculation of benchmark PPPs requires from each participating country a set of national annual average prices and a breakdown of national expenditure. The prices are used to derive price relatives for individual goods and services which are then averaged to obtain unweighted parities for groups of similar well-defined commodities – these commodity groups or expenditure categories are called "basic headings". The unweighted parities are subsequently combined using the breakdowns of national expenditures to derive weighted PPPs at various levels of aggregation cumulating in the overall PPPs for GDP.

The expenditure breakdown for 1990 for EUROSTAT countries consists of 257 basic headings. There are 216 basic headings for Private Final Consumption Expenditure, 9 for Government Final Consumption Expenditure and 30 for Gross Fixed Capital Formation (9 for construction, 21 for machinery and equipment). Increase in Stocks and Balance of Exports and Imports are treated as two basic headings and not broken down further. OECD countries use the same expenditure breakdown except that for Private Final Consumption Expenditure the breakdown is not as fine having only 160 basic headings.

The products selected for pricing have to be representative both of their basic heading and of the participating countries. Moreover, they have to be precisely defined to ensure that countries price and compare equivalent items. Consequently, for each basic heading, each participating country must nominate and define at least one product that is purchased sufficiently frequently for it to be representative of the expenditure by that country on the basic heading. To be included in the final selection, however, each product nominated must also be accepted by at least one other participating country and preferably by a country where the product, if not representative, is at least sold in large enough quantities for the price not to be untypical.

Since product lists were available from the price surveys for 1985, there was no need to repeat the lengthy negotiating process required to establish them. These lists were updated by EUROSTAT after consultations with its countries. The revised lists were subsequently enlarged by the OECD to include products that were representative of its countries for those basic headings where it appeared to be necessary.

The final product lists for the 1990 price surveys cover some 2 500 consumer goods and services, 30 occupations in government, education and health services, 250 types of equipment goods and 23 construction projects (8 residential buildings, 7 non-residential buildings and 8 civil engineering works). The construction projects are defined in bills of quantities that specify in detail the material and factor inputs.

Not all the products listed are available in all countries so not every product will be priced by every participating country. In a multilateral comparison, however, it is not necessary for a country to price all items because it is not necessary to calculate a direct binary parity for each pair of countries. A country need only price the most representative items (that is, its own products) and a share of the less representative items (that is, the products of other countries) for parities to be calculated, either directly or indirectly, between pairs of countries.

Data collection

At the time of drafting this note, the pricing of consumer goods and services has been completed. Five price surveys were held between Spring 1988 and Spring 1990 as follows:

- 1988-I Food, beverages and tobacco;
- 1988-II Major household appliances; transport equipment; recreational equipment;
- 1989-I House repairs; water, fuel and power; operation of transport equipment; transport and communication services; recreational services;
- 1989-II Clothing and footwear; textiles;
- 1990-I Furniture and floor coverings; glassware, tableware and utensils; household operation; personal care; restaurants and hotels; services nes.

Rents, insurances, medical goods (including pharmaceuticals) and medical services, however, were not covered in these price surveys. Instead they were subjects of special enquires undertaken either in mid-1989 or in early 1990.

The organisation of the price surveys for consumer items is the responsibility of the national statistical services. In EUROSTAT countries, the surveys are carried out in the capital cities. After each survey the individual price quotations collected are sent to EUROSTAT where they are converted to average prices. These average prices, which refer to the capital cities at the time of the survey, are subsequently adjusted by EUROSTAT to national annual prices using regional price indices to make them national and temporal price indices to centre them on 1990. The regional and temporal price indices are obtained from the countries.

OECD countries do not have the same resources available to them as EUROSTAT countries where the data collection is largely financed by EUROSTAT (except for Austria and Switzerland which, like OECD countries, finance their participation themselves). Consequently, the national statistical services of OECD countries make every effort to utilise the price data they collect for their consumer price indices (CPIs). Nonetheless, most OECD countries other than the United States find that some special pricing is still required and use their CPI infrastructures to obtain the additional prices. OECD countries provide the OECD with national average prices which the OECD subsequently centre on 1990 using the detailed temporal price indices supplied by the countries.

The collection of prices for Gross Fixed Capital Formation is undertaken in EUROSTAT countries by independent experts and funded by EUROSTAT. In OECD countries, however, responsibility for the collection of capital good prices rests with the national statistical services. Every effort is made to utilise the data they collect for their price indices relating to investment goods and construction, but special pricing is unavoidable. Usually the additional pricing for machinery and equipment is undertaken by the national statistical services, although in Canada it is contracted out to a private consultancy firm. Conversely, pricing the building and civil engineering projects is a problem for all national statistical services other than those of Canada and Norway. Usually the bills of quantities are completed by another government or quasi-government agency, although in Finland, New Zealand and the United States the pricing is done by private consultants.

The collection of prices for capital goods is currently underway and is expected to be completed by the end of October. The prices provided for machinery and equipment will be mid-year (July) prices for 1990. Similarly, for construction and civil engineering, the unit prices provided for the components detailed in the bill of quantities will be mid-1990 prices.

Compensation of employees working in selected occupations in government, health and education services is obtained by questionnaire from both groups of countries. The annual compensation in 1990 for each occupation is reported. This includes, in addition to gross salary, employer's contributions to social security, pension and similar schemes. Where such schemes are unfunded, the employer's contributions are inputed in line with the national accounting practices followed by the country. The survey of compensation of employees is scheduled to be completed by the end of September.

Expenditure data are also collected by questionnaire. Countries have been requested to provide by October 1990 a detailed breakdown of national expenditure by basic heading for the latest year available. In some cases this will be 1989, but usually it will be 1988 or even 1987. This breakdown will then be applied to the latest estimates for GDP and the main expenditure categories available for 1990 at the time of calculation.

Estimation and aggregation of parities

The calculation of PPPs is undertaken in two stages. First, there is the estimation of parities at the basic heading level; then, there is the aggregation of the basic heading parities up to the level of GDP. In the calculations for 1985, the Eltelo-Köves-Szulc (EKS) method was used to obtain the parities for the basic headings and the Geary-Khamis (GK) method was used to aggregate the basic heading parities. These calculations will be repeated for 1990.

In addition, the EKS method will also be used to aggregate the basic heading parities. This will provide users with two sets of results. Those obtained by the GK method will not be free of the Gerschenkron effect, but they will be additive and better suited to the analysis of price and volume structures across countries. Those obtained by the EKS method will not be additive, but the Gerschenkron effect will have been eliminated and they will be better suited for cross-country comparisons of the prices and volumes of individual aggregates.

III. Future developments

After 1990, benchmark PPPs will be calculated every three years instead of every five years as the cycle of price and expenditure surveys takes three years to complete. Until the new benchmark results are available, the PPPs for GDP and Private Final Consumption Expenditure will be updated annually by taking into account the relative rates of inflation in different countries as measured by the appropriate implicit price deflators.

The ultimate aim of the Programme, however, is to calculate PPPs on an annual basis. This will be done by using the new price data as they become available and by extrapolating the parities for basic headings for which no new price data are available with detailed price indices supplied by the countries. In fact this is already being done by EUROSTAT for its countries. It cannot be done as yet for OECD countries because prices for equipment and construction are only collected in benchmark years (EUROSTAT countries collect these prices each year) and sufficiently detailed and reliable price indices, that would enable benchmark parities for capital goods to be extrapolated, are not available.

WHERE TO OBTAIN OECD PUBLICATIONS – OÙ OBTENIR LES PUBLICATIONS DE L'OCDE

Argentina – Argentine
CARLOS HIRSCH S.R.L.
Galería Güemes, Florida 165, 4° Piso
1333 Buenos Aires Tel. 30.7122, 331.1787 y 331.2391
Telegram: Hirsch-Baires
Telex: 21112 UAPE-AR. Ref. s/2901
Telefax:(1)331-1787

Australia – Australie
D.A. Book (Aust.) Pty. Ltd.
648 Whitehorse Road, P.O.B 163
Mitcham, Victoria 3132 Tel. (03)873.4411
Telex: AA37911 DA BOOK
Telefax: (03)873.5679

Austria – Autriche
OECD Publications and Information Centre
Schedestrasse 7
DW-5300 Bonn 1 (Germany) Tel. (49.228)21.60.45
Telefax: (49.228)26.11.04

Gerold & Co.
Graben 31
Wien I Tel. (0222)533.50.14

Belgium – Belgique
Jean De Lannoy
Avenue du Roi 202
B-1060 Bruxelles Tel. (02)538.51.69/538.08.41
Telex: 63220 Telefax: (02) 538.08.41

Canada
Renouf Publishing Company Ltd.
1294 Algoma Road
Ottawa, ON K1B 3W8 Tel. (613)741.4333
Telex: 053-4783 Telefax: (613)741.5439
Stores:
61 Sparks Street
Ottawa, ON K1P 5R1 Tel. (613)238.8985
211 Yonge Street
Toronto, ON M5B 1M4 Tel. (416)363.3171

Federal Publications
165 University Avenue
Toronto, ON M5H 3B8 Tel. (416)581.1552
Telefax: (416)581.1743
Les Publications Fédérales
1185 rue de l'Université
Montréal, PQ H3B 3A7 Tel.(514)954-1633

Les Éditions La Liberté Inc.
3020 Chemin Sainte-Foy
Sainte-Foy, PQ G1X 3V6 Tel. (418)658.3763
Telefax: (418)658.3763

Denmark – Danemark
Munksgaard Export and Subscription Service
35, Nørre Søgade, P.O. Box 2148
DK-1016 København K Tel. (45 33)12.85.70
Telex: 19431 MUNKS DK Telefax: (45 33)12.93.87

Finland – Finlande
Akateeminen Kirjakauppa
Keskuskatu 1, P.O. Box 128
00100 Helsinki Tel. (358 0)12141
Telex: 125080 Telefax: (358 0)121.4441

France
OECD/OCDE
Mail Orders/Commandes par correspondance:
2, rue André-Pascal
75775 Paris Cédex 16 Tel. (33-1)45.24.82.00
Bookshop/Librairie:
33, rue Octave-Feuillet
75016 Paris Tel. (33-1)45.24.81.67
(33-1)45.24.81.81
Telex: 620 160 OCDE
Telefax: (33-1)45.24.85.00 (33-1)45.24.81.76

Librairie de l'Université
12a, rue Nazareth
13100 Aix-en-Provence Tel. 42.26.18.08
Telefax : 42.26.63.26

Germany – Allemagne
OECD Publications and Information Centre
Schedestrasse 7
DW-5300 Bonn 1 Tel. (0228)21.60.45
Telefax: (0228)26.11.04

Greece – Grèce
Librairie Kauffmann
28 rue du Stade
105 64 Athens Tel. 322.21.60
Telex: 218187 LIKA Gr

Hong Kong
Swindon Book Co. Ltd.
13 - 15 Lock Road
Kowloon, Hong Kong Tel. 366.80.31
Telex: 50 441 SWIN HX Telefax: 739.49.75

Iceland – Islande
Mál Mog Menning
Laugavegi 18, Pósthólf 392
121 Reykjavik Tel. 15199/24240

India – Inde
Oxford Book and Stationery Co.
Scindia House
New Delhi 110001 Tel. 331.5896/5308
Telex: 31 61990 AM IN
Telefax: (11)332.5993
17 Park Street
Calcutta 700016 Tel. 240832

Indonesia – Indonésie
Pdii-Lipi
P.O. Box 269/JKSMG/88
Jakarta 12790 Tel. 583467
Telex: 62 875

Ireland – Irlande
TDC Publishers – Library Suppliers
12 North Frederick Street
Dublin 1 Tel. 744835/749677
Telex: 33530 TDCP EI Telefax: 748416

Italy – Italie
Libreria Commissionaria Sansoni
Via Benedetto Fortini, 120/10
Casella Post. 552
50125 Firenze Tel. (055)64.54.15
Telex: 570466 Telefax: (055)64.12.57
Via Bartolini 29
20155 Milano Tel. 36.50.83
La diffusione delle pubblicazioni OCSE viene assicurata dalle principali librerie ed anche da:

Editrice e Libreria Herder
Piazza Montecitorio 120
00186 Roma Tel. 679.46.28
Telex: NATEL I 621427

Libreria Hoepli
Via Hoepli 5
20121 Milano Tel. 86.54.46
Telex: 31.33.95 Telefax: (02)805.28.86

Libreria Scientifica
Dott. Lucio de Biasio 'Aeiou'
Via Meravigli 16
20123 Milano Tel. 805.68.98
Telefax: 800175

Japan – Japon
OECD Publications and Information Centre
Landic Akasaka Building
2-3-4 Akasaka, Minato-ku
Tokyo 107 Tel. (81.3)3586.2016
Telefax: (81.3)3584.7929

Korea – Corée
Kyobo Book Centre Co. Ltd.
P.O. Box 1658, Kwang Hwa Moon
Seoul Tel. (REP)730.78.91
Telefax: 735.0030

Malaysia/Singapore – Malaisie/Singapour
Co-operative Bookshop Ltd.
University of Malaya
P.O. Box 1127, Jalan Pantai Baru
59700 Kuala Lumpur
Malaysia Tel. 756.5000/756.5425
Telefax: 757.3661

Information Publications Pte. Ltd.
Pei-Fu Industrial Building
24 New Industrial Road No. 02-06
Singapore 1953 Tel. 283.1786/283.1798
Telefax: 284.8875

Netherlands – Pays-Bas
SDU Uitgeverij
Christoffel Plantijnstraat 2
Postbus 20014
2500 EA's-Gravenhage Tel. (070 3)78.99.11
Voor bestellingen: Tel. (070 3)78.98.80
Telex: 32486 stdru Telefax: (070 3)47.63.51

New Zealand – Nouvelle-Zélande
GP Publications Ltd.
Customer Services
33 The Esplanade - P.O. Box 38-900
Petone, Wellington
Tel. (04)685-555 Telefax: (04)685-333

Norway – Norvège
Narvesen Info Center - NIC
Bertrand Narvesens vei 2
P.O. Box 6125 Etterstad
0602 Oslo 6 Tel. (02)57.33.00
Telex: 79668 NIC N Telefax: (02)68.19.01

Pakistan
Mirza Book Agency
65 Shahrah Quaid-E-Azam
Lahore 3 Tel. 66839
Telex: 44886 UBL PK. Attn: MIRZA BK

Portugal
Livraria Portugal
Rua do Carmo 70-74
Apart. 2681
1117 Lisboa Codex Tel.: 347.49.82/3/4/5
Telefax: (01) 347.02.64

Singapore/Malaysia – Singapour/Malaisie
See Malaysia/Singapore" – Voir «Malaisie/Singapour»

Spain – Espagne
Mundi-Prensa Libros S.A.
Castelló 37, Apartado 1223
Madrid 28001 Tel. (91) 431.33.99
Telex: 49370 MPLI Telefax: 575.39.98

Libreria Internacional AEDOS
Consejo de Ciento 391
08009-Barcelona Tel. (93) 301.86.15
Telefax: (93) 317.01.41

Sri Lanka
Centre for Policy Research
c/o Mercantile Credit Ltd.
55, Janadhipathi Mawatha
Colombo 1 Tel. 438471-9, 440346
Telex: 21138 VAVALEX CE Telefax: 94.1.448900

Sweden – Suède
Fritzes Fackboksföretaget
Box 16356, S 103 27 STH
Regeringsgatan 12
DS Stockholm Tel. (08)23.89.00
Telex: 12387 Telefax: (08)20.50.21
Subscription Agency/Abonnements:
Wennergren-Williams AB
Nordenflychtsvagen 74
Box 30004
104 25 Stockholm Tel. (08)13.67.00
Telex: 19937 Telefax: (08)618.62.36

Switzerland – Suisse
OECD Publications and Information Centre
Schedestrasse 7
DW-5300 Bonn 1 (Germany) Tel. (49.228)21.60.45
Telefax: (49.228)26.11.04

Librairie Payot
6 rue Grenus
1211 Genève 11 Tel. (022)731.89.50
Telex: 28356
Subscription Agency – Service des Abonnements
Naville S.A.
7, rue Lévrier
1201 Genève Tél.: (022) 732.24.00
Telefax: (022) 738.48.03

Maditec S.A.
Chemin des Palettes 4
1020 Renens/Lausanne Tel. (021)635.08.65
Telefax: (021)635.07.80

United Nations Bookshop/Librairie des Nations-Unies
Palais des Nations
1211 Genève 10 Tel. (022)734.60.11 (ext. 48.72)
Telex: 289696 (Attn: Sales) Telefax: (022)733.98.79

Taiwan – Formose
Good Faith Worldwide Int'l. Co. Ltd.
9th Floor, No. 118, Sec. 2
Chung Hsiao E. Road
Taipei Tel. 391.7396/391.7397
Telefax: (02) 394.9176

Thailand – Thaïlande
Suksit Siam Co. Ltd.
1715 Rama IV Road, Samyan
Bangkok 5 Tel. 251.1630

Turkey – Turquie
Kültur Yayinlari Is-Türk Ltd. Sti.
Atatürk Bulvari No. 191/Kat. 21
Kavaklidere/Ankara Tel. 25.07.60
Dolmabahce Cad. No. 29
Besiktas/Istanbul Tel. 160.71.88
Telex: 43482B

United Kingdom – Royaume-Uni
HMSO
Gen. enquiries Tel. (071) 873 0011
Postal orders only:
P.O. Box 276, London SW8 5DT
Personal Callers HMSO Bookshop
49 High Holborn, London WC1V 6HB
Telex: 297138 Telefax: 071 873 8463
Branches at: Belfast, Birmingham, Bristol, Edinburgh, Manchester

United States – États-Unis
OECD Publications and Information Centre
2001 L Street N.W., Suite 700
Washington, D.C. 20036-4095 Tel. (202)785.6323
Telefax: (202)785.0350

Venezuela
Libreria del Este
Avda F. Miranda 52, Aptdo. 60337
Edificio Galipán
Caracas 106 Tel. 951.1705/951.2307/951.1297
Telegram: Libreste Caracas

Yugoslavia – Yougoslavie
Jugoslovenska Knjiga
Knez Mihajlova 2, P.O. Box 36
Beograd Tel.: (011)621.992
Telex: 12466 jk bgd Telefax: (011)625.970

Orders and inquiries from countries where Distributors have not yet been appointed should be sent to: OECD Publications Service, 2 rue André-Pascal, 75775 Paris Cedex 16, France.

Les commandes provenant de pays où l'OCDE n'a pas encore désigné de distributeur devraient être adressées à : OCDE, Service des Publications, 2, rue André-Pascal, 75775 Paris Cédex 16, France.

75490–1/91

OECD PUBLICATIONS, 2 rue André-Pascal, 75775 PARIS CEDEX 16
PRINTED IN FRANCE
(14 91 04 1) ISBN 92-64-13486-7 - No. 45543 1991